Sustaining Professionalism

Edited by Patricia Byrd
and Gayle Nelson

Professional Development in
Language Education Series.
Volume 3

Tim Murphey. Series Editor

TESOL

Teachers of English to Speakers of Other Languages, Inc.

Typeset in Giovanni and Bunky
by Capitol Communication Systems, Inc., Crofton, Maryland USA
Printed by Kirby Lithographic Company, Inc., Arlington, Virginia USA

Teachers of English to Speakers of Other Languages, Inc.
700 South Washington Street, Suite 200
Alexandria, Virginia 22314 USA
Tel 703-836-0774 • Fax 703-836-6447 • E-mail info@tesol.org • http://www.tesol.org/

Director of Publishing: Paul G. Gibbs
Managing Editor: Marilyn Kupetz
Copy Editor: Marcia Annis
Additional Reader: Ellen Garshick
Cover Design: Capitol Communication Systems, Inc.

ISBN 1931185115
Library of Congress Control No. 2002116677

Contents

Series Editor's Preface

TESOL's Professional Development in Language Education series was conceived by the TESOL Publications Committee as a way to provide a wide array of choices to teachers for continuing their development throughout their careers. The series is based on the recognition that those who contribute most to the profession and to their students' learning see their own continual learning and development as crucial to their work. Such professionals regularly challenge their beliefs, their methods, and the status quo; they seek out and explore a variety of ways to teach and learn. In doing so they not only contribute to their own professional development, but also create a contagious wave of excitement that entrains colleagues and communities of learners.

Professional development is the raison d'être of professional associations like TESOL, and thus we need to think more consciously about how we do it and challenge ourselves to seek better and more effective ways to develop ourselves. Besides making efforts to improve themselves and their students, TESOL professionals also seek to stimulate the profession and give back to the field. All the contributors to this series are sharing in this effort by offering insightful and innovative ways of professional development.

Volume 1 in the series, *Becoming Contributing Professionals,* is focused on what new teachers can do to continue their development. It seeks to inspire them to build on the excitement of initial education and incorporate continual development into their lives. A common thread in all three volumes, started here, is that technology can play a significant role in TESOL professionals' continual development.

Volume 2, *Extending Professional Contributions,* highlights midcareer professionals and looks at ways they have sought to continue developing. Most apparent in this volume is the amount of development that comes from collaboration with other teachers and researchers. Professional development is immensely richer when done with others in a community in which excitement and ideas grow exponentially with colleagues.

Volume 3, *Sustaining Professionalism,* looks at ways that more seasoned professionals have continued to develop professionally. Many of these chapters reveal how personal lives are intertwined with professional lives and how many professional decisions have major consequences for life histories, taking us to new places and giving us profound experiences. It is gratifying to see how we as TESOL professionals can continue to innovate and rise to challenges throughout our careers.

These three volumes are testimony to the diversity and courage in the TESOL profession. Although the contents of the three volumes flow across the different stages of a career in TESOL, all TESOL professionals can learn from many of the chapters in each volume and can learn how to stimulate the professional development of their colleagues. I am excited to think of the impact this series will have on many teachers and the continual quality of TESOL as it offers professional development globally.

Tim Murphey

Acknowledgment

We would like to thank Kelly McClure for her careful reading and editing, and for making time when deadlines approached.

Introduction

Patricia Byrd and Gayle Nelson

Over the years, we have observed some colleagues struggle to maintain the emotional and intellectual drive that brought them into the field while other colleagues continue to thrive. As a result of these observations, we approached this book motivated by a desire to explore the strategies available to TESOL professionals for continued growth and renewal. We sought participation from teachers who have been in the field for many years and who remain active, interested, and excited about their work. We asked them these questions: How have you done it? What keeps you interested? What do you recommend to other teachers?

As we have read through the authors' answers to our questions, we see that ultimately the answers depend on individual interests, talents, and personalities. There is no one-size-fits-all method for keeping teachers excited about their careers. After considering many themes in these chapters, we identified six major clusters of opportunities for TESOL professionals seeking change in their professional lives: (a) remaining a teacher-scholar, (b) becoming a writer, (c) moving into administration, (d) creating teacher development programs and workshops, (e) getting away, and (f) taking political action.

The first four chapters illustrate strategies for change and renewal used by teachers and scholars who have stayed focused on teaching and scholarship through the years. Clark (chapter 1) gives a heartwarming description of the transformations, detours, and affirmations in her career that have led to her continuing as a classroom teacher. She suggests practical ways to build confidence, connections, and commitment into professional development activities. Cohen (chapter 2) gives advice on building a career as a researcher-scholar-teacher using methods that have led to recognition of his achievements by his university. Tanner (chapter 3) vividly discusses her feelings and strategies when required to develop a teaching portfolio, a task we as TESOL professionals often require of students. Daloğlu (chapter 4) shows how a university professor of TESOL can renew connections to the high school EFL classroom and reenergize an academic career by developing a drama festival that motivates students to study English.

The next three chapters illustrate ways that writing and publication can energize careers in TESOL. Averill (chapter 5) provides an insider's tips on developing skills at writing grant proposals that get funded. In chapter 6, Murphy shows how the new work of editing a book enriched his life as a scholar-teacher. Then, in chapter 7, Grant explains her gradual move away from teaching to materials writing and advises TESOL professionals on how to make a similar transition.

In chapters 8 and 9, two academics discuss the benefits and challenges of moving from the classroom into administration. Although they work in different countries with somewhat different expectations of teachers and administrators, Stapa (chapter 8) and Smith (chapter 9) give practical advice for teachers who think that taking on administrative roles might be a good next step in their careers. The next two chapters show classroom language teachers learning to be teacher educators and developing skills at organizing effective training for other language teachers. Spector-Cohen, Wexler, and Kol (chapter 10) demonstrate what can happen for a program and for teachers when they decide to build a system for ongoing curricular revision. Beaven (chapter 11) describes her efforts to train teachers to give effective workshop presentations through a teacher education workshop that she developed.

Chapters 12, 13, and 14 prove the value of getting away from it all. Seymour (chapter 12) describes her decision to take a sabbatical and study an area of the curriculum that interested her. She then discusses the changes in her department and her institution that connected her study to a major revision of the ESL curriculum. Conrad (chapter 13) discusses her move from a secure job to a new location that better fit her own personal needs. She gives practical advice about making the decision as well as preparing for and dealing with the resulting changes. Nelson (chapter 14) weaves her way through personal and professional reasoning to opt for a Fulbright sabbatical in Mexico and to take her 15-year-old son with her. She vividly recounts the visit's impact on her personal and professional life.

We close the book with Braine's discussion of his leadership of and participation in the development of TESOL's Nonnative English Speakers in TESOL caucus (chapter 15). He explains how personal history can inspire a commitment to the development of the profession through effective political action. This final chapter challenges and inspires teachers to find ways to be more powerful—for themselves and the students they teach—by learning how their system works and how they can influence and perhaps even control that system.

For these long-term professionals, the ultimate answer to having a long, satisfying career seems to have been to develop a skill for recognizing and seizing satisfying opportunities that fit their individual personalities. We conclude this introduction with a checklist of opportunities suggested in the chapters as a convenient summary for those seeking ideas for change and renewal (see p. 12).

Contributors

Patricia Byrd (patbyrd@gsu.edu) is a professor in the Department of Applied Linguistics and ESL at Georgia State University in Atlanta, in the United States, where she teaches graduate courses in English grammar; corpus linguistics; and materials design, development, and publication. She sustains her career through experimenting with the

✓	A Checklist of Activities to Enhance Careers Over Time
	Find the time to do one project each year, for example, give a presentation at a TESOL conference or write a book review.
	Develop or improve a skill, for example, learn to give workshops or study the work of people who are experienced workshop presenters.
	Analyze the career track required for success at your institution, and focus on achieving those goals.
	Find a research area that excites you and start working on it. Review the literature, sketch out possible research designs, seek research grants, and organize your schedule to include time for this work at least weekly.
	Prepare an extensive teaching portfolio, and use it to plan new approaches to old courses.
	Network outside your university by meeting with schoolteachers in your area to create activities, such as a drama festival or a student publication.
	Learn to write grants and manage funded projects.
	Edit a book.
	Become a published materials writer.
	Write reviews for TESOL publications at the local, state, regional, national, and international levels.
	Take on an administrative position.
	Seek training for administrative work through professional organizations.
	Become active in TESOL or another professional organization.
	With other teachers, create a program to improve your department.
	Become a teacher educator.
	Study a new topic, such as teacher development or program administration.
	Seek opportunities for professional leave, and use them for study and reflection on some topic of importance to you, your program, or your department.
	Apply for a Fulbright grant, or take other opportunities to teach or study in another country.
	Admit that the fit between you and your current job is OK but not all that it could be, and seek a new job.
	Figure out the TESOL system, and strategize with colleagues over ways to influence the association and improve the profession.
	Analyze the system where you work (e.g., the school, department, college or university, local school system). Take on committee work or other tasks to develop skills at influencing the decisions made about your classes and students you teach.

use of computers in teaching and research and through writing and editing materials.

Gayle Nelson (gaylenelson@gsu.edu) is chair of and professor in the Department of Applied Linguistics and ESL at Georgia State University in Atlanta, in the United States. She conducts research on cultural issues related to second language acquisition and teaches intercultural communication. She sustains herself professionally by conducting research, teaching abroad, and furthering international education.

On Remaining a Teacher: Transformations, Detours, and Affirmations

Carol Clark

Narrative

> "Did you really throw your shoe across the room and make us write about it?"
> "You took us to see *Macbeth*. I loved Shakespeare after that."
> "I remember when you read us 'The Scarlet Ibis' and you cried at the end."

Thirty years later, each of us had vivid memories of Mrs. Newton's 11th- and 12th-grade English classes. I was back in Seattle for the first time in years, and my friend Betty had arranged a small get-together for our high school friends. We had planned the event by e-mail and decided to invite our former high school English teacher.

Each of us remembered different aspects of her class and debated whether she had really thrown that shoe (she had). When she arrived that day, she was as vigorous as ever, with her red hair, penetrating eyes, and broad grin. As memories were confirmed, a common denominator emerged—Mrs. Newton had greatly influenced our lives, forging links between the real world and our writing, helping us appreciate great literature, guiding us in choosing colleges, and, most importantly, making us aware of our potential. Happily, that evening provided a chance to let her know how much she had meant to us.

As I think about myself as a teacher, I am doubly inspired by this special woman. She was one of the first of several outstanding people who modeled the best of the teaching profession and encouraged me to become and remain a teacher. Of course, I have a different personality and style in the classroom (yes, I take students to see Shakespeare plays and sometimes read them stories aloud; no, I have not thrown my shoe across the room as a writing prompt). Yet thinking about the variety and creativity of Mrs. Newton's teaching methods, the rigor of her assessments, and her impact on her students gives me a high standard to aim for and motivates me when my teaching spirit flags. All teachers need people like her to serve as models. We also need to contribute to the growth of other teachers in a recursive, dynamic process in order to sustain ourselves and continually renew the profession.

Description

When I compare myself as a teacher in my first year of teaching with myself as a teacher today, I notice many small changes that led to some gradual but major transformations. Most professional transformations involve reciprocal relationships within the profession. At the beginning, as a new teacher trying to absorb the requisite knowledge in my subject area; organize it into lessons; and manage the factors of time, space, and student behavior in the classroom, I relied heavily on what I could take from others in the profession. They included my own past teachers, curriculum developers and materials writers, more experienced teachers in my department, administrators, and academics and teacher educators at in-service workshops. Although as beginning teachers most of us rely on the work of others, we later begin to combine the best practices available from the profession with our own styles and bring about changes in our teaching. As we grow as teachers, we need to add our own contributions in a dynamic relationship with colleagues.

This first transformation, *from teacher to professional*, began during a conversation with a friend who had recently presented a paper at a conference. Although she complained about the massive amount of work she had done to conduct her research and prepare her paper, she articulated a very simple but powerful concept. As a professional, her goal was to conduct one extra project, such as a research paper, conference presentation, or in-service workshop, outside of her classroom teaching every year. Although we were not in publish-or-perish, tenure-track positions, she had decided that such a practice could only help her grow as a teacher and maximize her chances of being rehired.

However, the reason to contribute to the profession beyond our classrooms goes even deeper. The words *profession, professional*, or even *professor* are all based on the word *profess*, meaning to affirm, declare, or admit to, openly and freely. Thus, as members of a profession, we have the obligation to go beyond the walls of our own classrooms, comfortable as they may be, and contribute to the development and knowledge of other educators.

As I internalized and began to practice this fundamental concept about professionalism, I became inspired. When I made my first presentation to departmental colleagues about a cross-cultural language acquisition project, I felt I had finally become a full-fledged member of the department. The next major step was to participate in our in-service program. Finally, after having dreamed of going to a TESOL convention for more than 10 years, a colleague mentored me through the preparation of my first TESOL demonstration. Attending that first convention was invigorating and challenging. I returned to Cairo full of fresh ideas for my program, but also realized how much more there was to explore and learn from others.

So the first transformation evolved. I started with the goal of completing one extra project a year 17 years ago; now, I work on three or four a year, sometimes more. Over time, linking what I was doing in the classroom to the larger professional world got easier. With practice, writing proposals, designing professional presentations, and writing up findings became less daunting tasks. One small project led to another, and through each one, I met and worked with different people and began to build a body of work. Once I was willing to *profess*, I was invited to do so, and this dynamic process enabled me to set and achieve new goals, develop new interests, and establish new links with colleagues, which helped sustain me.

Another important transformation, *from being teacher-centered to becoming student-centered*, gave me new energy and focus and came, surprisingly, later in my career. Rather than a shift in practices, this transformation involved a shift in perspective and attitude. Its impetus was a passage in *Growing Minds: On Becoming a Teacher* (Kohl, 1984). In this book, Kohl describes his motivation for choosing teaching as a profession. He compares the growth a teacher promotes in students to adding new parts to buildings that are always under construction. The following lines in particular struck a resounding chord in me:

> Buildings do not build themselves, but people do. Understanding the complex relationships between self-growth and nurturing growth is essential to becoming a good teacher. Further, the love of nurturing and observing growth in others is essential to sustaining a life in teaching. This implies that no matter what you teach or how you present yourself to students, you have to be on the learners' side and to believe that they can and will grow during the time you are together. (pp. 4–5)

Internalizing this key idea about teaching shifted my focus in the classroom from myself to the students and their growth. Suddenly my repertoire of knowledge, materials, and activities became not just tools of the trade but a rich source on which I could draw to tap into what students cared about and needed. Instead of worrying about how to fill the class hour, I began to worry about how to get through enough of the material that students needed in the little time we had. With this new focus came a new sense of curiosity and excitement about what students would think, write about, and express in class about the texts and ideas we were exploring. This attitude shift on my part met with a welcome response in students, and another sustaining transformation was underway.

Like booster rockets, these two transformations have carried me through 3 decades of teaching. But they also combined with two other factors: the detours I took and the affirmations I began to discover.

My detours led me from 13 years of language teaching to 5 years of program administration at the American University in Cairo (AUC), and then to 6 years of teacher education and administration in a large, national-level teacher education project funded by the U.S. Agency for International Development. When that project closed, I returned to language teaching at AUC. This variety of professional experiences at institutional and national levels with different colleagues has in turn led to another shift in viewpoint. I now see myself not only as a teacher or administrator or teacher trainer, but as an educator, who may be called on to fulfill any of these roles at different times. My career no longer seems to be a vertical hierarchical ladder but instead seems to be a river, which can branch out in one direction for a while and then return to the main stream. In addition, the new skills and perspectives acquired during my detours into administration and teacher education have enriched and informed my classroom teaching.

A final factor that has sustained me in teaching has been what I call *affirmations*, the sense that I am doing the right thing for myself and the students, and that my practices are shared by other professionals and supported by research. In a sense, Kohl's (1984) articulation of learning to love the growth in students affirmed my own deep-seated beliefs and set off a major transformation. Affirmations can come from students—from the delight you feel in their achievements and from their feedback—from like-minded colleagues, professional readings, and conferences; even from movies, such as the final scene in *Mr. Holland's Opus* (Herek, 1995), when students perform his symphony and say, "There is not a life in this room that you have not touched. Each of us is a better person because of you. We are your symphony, Mr. Holland . . . we are the music of your life."

Such powerful and moving moments affirm us, reminding us why we continue to work with students. These affirmations can nourish our inner lives as teachers, lead to new detours or transformations, and help sustain us professionally.

Steps

In sustaining a career as an educator, three interconnecting factors help one to stay dynamic and refreshed as a professional: confidence, connection, and commitment.

Build Confidence

Beginning teachers often feel they have nothing new or different to say to others in the profession. As you begin to experience success in the classroom, think of ways to contribute to the success of others that will help build their professional confidence.

1. Try new materials sent to you or your institution or new activities that colleagues recommend.

2. Write a review of new materials or a book, and submit it to a regional, national, or international newsletter or journal.

3. Develop new materials and activities to fit the needs of students or to fill a gap in your program. Pool materials in a resource room, and share them with your colleagues.

4. Find a mentor who has given workshops, and collaborate to plan and present one.

5. Read, read, read: about other teachers' journeys, the latest research in your area of interest, or students' cultures.

6. Every few years, look for a new inspirational paradigm to inform your teaching and spur your professional growth. Other chapters in this book suggest a range of options.

7. Formulate driving questions about your teaching, students, or your methods, and design an action research project to answer them. Participate more as your confidence builds.

Develop Connections

The following are some ways to communicate and connect with others in the teaching profession.

1. Find mentors and colleagues who share your passion for teaching and learning. Listen to their stories, ask questions, and explore answers together.

2. Join several professional organizations. Local TESOL affiliates are excellent places to begin. Add other organizations to broaden your perspectives, such as the Association for Supervision and Curriculum Development (ASCD), or to deepen your focus in one area, such as the Computer Assisted Language Instruction Consortium (CALICO).

3. Attend conferences whenever possible; investigate areas for presentations and service. Find ways to volunteer so that you can make new connections.

4. Join a professional online discussion list or forum, publish in an e-journal or on a language learning Web site, or take a course over the Internet.

5. Seek variety and breadth in your professional activities. Make a detour into teacher education, administration, or materials writing. Change conferences or your conference focus; shift from leading workshops to writing articles, or from individual to collaborative work. Find new audiences and roles.

Make a Commitment

Make a conscious commitment to yourself to sustaining a life as a professional educator. The following suggestions can help you fulfill this commitment.

1. Set new goals regularly. Do not be discouraged if it takes a while to reach them.

2. Attend refresher courses every few years. Take advantage of pre- and postconference institutes and summer programs.

3. Remember to look back along the road and encourage other teachers who are just beginning.

Conclusion

Sustaining a life in teaching is not easy. Many competent young teachers are lost to the profession every year. In a profession that deals with the intangibles of human learning and growth, it is easy to become too overwhelmed, discouraged, or cynical to continue. We often fail to see the full impact of our teaching on students' lives in the little time we have with them. In the EFL/ESL profession in particular, with its international opportunities for teachers and mobile student populations, most of us are not as fortunate as my high school English teacher, Mrs. Newton, or Mr. Holland, whose former students gathered years later to acknowledge their influence. However, education is one of the most rewarding professions because it requires us to continue our own growth as well as to develop that of our students. Through our contributions to the profession, we reaffirm our dedication to the development of human potential and sustain ourselves and one another in the profession.

Resources

Association for Supervision and Curriculum Development (ASCD). http://www.ascd.org/

> ASCD provides resources for administrators, trainers, and curriculum developers for K–12 schools, including information on current educational trends in U.S. schools.

Computer Assisted Language Instruction Consortium (CALICO). http://www.calico.org/

> CALICO focuses on the use of computers in modern language instruction.

Herek, S. (Director). (1995). *Mr. Holland's opus* [Motion picture]. United States: Hollywood Pictures.

> This film features a would-be composer who becomes a high school music teacher and learns many lessons from his students and his family over a 30-year career. Clear dialogue and a focus on family and school issues make this a good film to show to ESL/EFL students.

Kohl, H. R. (1984). *Growing minds: On becoming a teacher.* New York: Harper & Row.

> This narrative combines educational theory with the autobiography of a master teacher-writer-educational reformer. Kohl originally found fame in the 1960s as the author of *The Open Classroom*, describing a controversial approach to creatively inspiring disadvantaged elementary students to learn.

Contributor

Carol Clark (cclark@aucegypt.edu) teaches EFL to graduate and undergraduate students in the Intensive English Program of the English Language Institute at the American University in Cairo, Egypt. She has taught ESL/EFL in Mexico, the United States, Turkey, and Egypt, and English literature and methodology at Egyptian universities. She has also worked in program administration and teacher education.

2 Becoming "Scholar of the College"

Andrew D. Cohen

Narrative

Every year, the University of Minnesota's College of Liberal Arts selects faculty for a Scholar of the College award to acknowledge their outstanding achievements. The award carries with it a 3-year research stipend. Much to my surprise and satisfaction, I received the 2002 award along with four colleagues.

My reflections on why I received this award constitute my contribution to this volume. Here I romp through my areas of academic endeavor in an effort to tease out some dos and don'ts that may benefit others who are aspiring to become established scholars in their own right.

Description

My scholarship efforts have fallen into three areas, partly by design but partly by accident. First, I have worked in the area of language learning strategies, focusing on success at academic study through language immersion (at the elementary school and university levels) and on strategies for learning speech acts (i.e., utterances that serve a function in communication, such as apologies and complaints) in another language. My fascination with language learning strategies is an artifact of my own efforts at learning 11 languages (see Cohen, 1998).

Second, I have worked in the area of language assessment ever since I was assigned to teach an introduction to language assessment course at the University of California, Los Angeles (UCLA), in the early 1970s as well as being responsible for UCLA's ESL Placement Exam.

Third, I have dealt with issues of research methods in applied linguistic studies, such as the use of verbal reports to enhance our understanding of language acquisition. What characterizes my writings is that the topics were, for the most part, of my own choosing (see Step 3 below).

Steps

The nine operating principles for becoming a scholar offered here correspond to the following categories: university teaching, taking on administrative roles, choosing a research topic, preparing grant proposals, conducting a research study, giving talks, writing for publication, getting organized, and maintaining a life.

1. Choose the university courses you teach carefully. If you want to be productive as a scholar, your teaching must support your research and writing efforts.

   - If possible, select courses in your research area that you really want to teach. If that is not possible, you may at least be able to select days, times, and venues for the courses in ways that help your research (e.g., set a class schedule that leaves larger chunks of time for research). For a course on research methods in second language acquisition (SLA), I negotiated a change from a dungeon-like room, remembering how depressing it had been to teach there previously.

   - Within your courses, find topics you would want to research. You may even be able to find graduate or undergraduate students who would be thrilled to assist you. A language immersion study emerged from a course I was teaching in SLA. Five undergraduates volunteered to assist me, and two even got university funding (see Parker, Heitzman, Fjerstad, Babbs, & Cohen, 1995).

- If possible, conduct each class with the same zeal as when delivering a conference presentation. I gained this insight when I found that some of my class sessions were not motivating students to engage the material, at a time when I was having better success at delivering conference presentations. So I started preparing for class sessions as if they were conference presentations, including interactive resources, such as Microsoft PowerPoint presentations, to enhance them, which improved my course ratings.

2. Take on administrative roles cautiously. Remember, you were probably hired primarily to be an academician. If thrust into an administrative role, you may be asked to do things you were not trained to do, such as tactfully hiring and firing your colleagues. If you devote your time to administration (e.g., reviewing applicants to your program, meeting with colleagues on programmatic issues, interviewing candidates for staff positions), when will you find time for research and writing?

3. Be careful when choosing topics to research and write about. Especially after publishing something noteworthy, you may get requests to continue in that area. For example, a colleague may suggest collaborating on some research project. Before making a commitment, ask yourself whether you are really motivated to see it through to completion. Commit yourself only to something you are passionate about. Avoid getting stuck in a research or writing project that lacks sustained interest for you.

4. Take the preparation of a grant proposal seriously. Proposals require planning and long-term thinking. They need to be submitted 6 months or more before notification of grant awards and almost a year before the granting period begins. You should therefore plan a 2- or 3-year study 2 years before it would begin. You may also want to consider the programs and technological support that will be available several years in the future. Give yourself lots of lead time to prepare (e.g., at least a year before the submission deadline), and enlist the support of others so as not to overlook crucial details by attempting to do

everything on your own. At the University of Minnesota, we were fortunate to have had the help of a full-time grant writer. In preparing the first major grant we obtained, he conducted a content analysis of previous winning grant proposals. He instructed us in what issues to stress and the appropriate language to use. Our proposal was rated as the top candidate for that cycle.

5. Design a research study that is destined to succeed. How do you find the time to conduct the research while teaching full time, serving on committees, attending conferences, and attempting to publish papers and books?

- Hire the right research assistant, a self-starter, who shows initiative and can be relied on to work independently with minimal supervision.

- Be aware of the research requirements governing work with human subjects as stipulated by your university and any public schools involved. You may need to present detailed descriptions of the stages of the study, the instruments, the research methods, and so forth, as well as obtain permission from subjects and their legal guardians (if they are minors). You will also need to develop a time line for activities so that everything goes smoothly.

- Do not begin the study until you have official approval from the human subjects office. I made the mistake of attending a meeting in Paris with the expectation that a summer study would get approval. Four research assistants (RAs) were already hired and poised for action. Much to my horror, I learned while abroad that the human subjects committee had found several minor points in the proposal that needed clarification. Unfortunately, I had already instructed an RA to send letters of consent to over 600 parents. When two of the parents called the human subjects office to complain about the study, the office angrily ordered the termination of the study. The study was conducted successfully the following summer, but only after a painful ordeal.

- Remember that research in the real world always involves glitches (see Cumming & Swain, 1989). For instance, if one of the teachers in an instructional intervention study is absent for an extended period, you may need to abandon the study in that classroom. This recently happened to me in a study of a fifth-grade Spanish language class where the substitute teachers spoke only English.

- Although the joys of doing research outweigh the possible glitches, avoid as many glitches as possible through advance planning.

6. Do not overcommit yourself to giving local talks and national conference presentations. You may be so flattered to be asked that you neglect to consider carefully the demands of preparing and traveling and the consequences of being away (e.g., classes missed with or without makeup, a backlog of e-mail and regular mail).

- Make sure trips are worth taking. Do not be abashed about discussing the honorarium, per diem, and other issues. Do not feel obligated to perform your scholarly duties without remuneration. Other professionals, such as doctors, lawyers, and engineers, do not generally provide free services, so why should you?

- Schedule trips so that you have recovery time in between.

- If possible, build in some vacation time around your conference, especially if it takes place somewhere you have always wanted to visit. To be a productive scholar, you need time to play.

7. Be serious about allotting yourself time to write. Finding this time is perhaps the biggest challenge of all.

- Some colleagues set aside a day just for writing (e.g., Fridays); however, doing so at the office may be difficult due to meetings and other interruptions. Some block off portions of the day to write, such as early in the morning or late at night.

- Some devote weekends to writing. I take a break from academic work from Friday evening through all of Saturday (unless I am at a conference). I make Sunday a work day.

- An ideal time to write is during a nonteaching sabbatical. I wrote my last solo-authored book on such a sabbatical as a visiting scholar, first at the University of Hawai'i and then at Tel Aviv University. Uninterrupted time is invaluable when writing an entire book or even an article or book chapter.

- Writing with one or more colleagues can have real advantages. When one or more of the coauthors experience a lack of motivation, energy, or time, the other(s) can push. Even if you do not actually write with others, having colleagues at your home institution or elsewhere read a draft of your writing before you submit it for publication can be beneficial. Although you may receive unwanted feedback (especially if it calls for extensive revision), the suggestions could be crucial to getting the work published.

- The final caveat is to write something you want to write. A collection of scholarly publications emerges over the years from writing articles, chapters, and books because you wanted to write them.

8. Create an effective system of organization. I have received training in time management and office organization and began using a management book before they became popular. In addition, I have an organizational board on the wall with categories (e.g., writings, data analysis, courses, trips, talks, administration, proposals, readings) under which I place stick-on notes with reminders about things to do. I remove each stick-on note when the item has been handled. I can therefore see at a glance the pieces I need to write, the talks I need to give, and the trips I need to take. The board helps me avoid double booking and lets me see how many writing commitments are already on my plate before I add another. Finally, I use stacked trays as an inbox to keep track of letters and other documents so that I can see at a glance what I need to respond to. Consequently, nothing gets buried and forgotten.

9. If at all possible, have a rich life outside of academia. If you do not want to burn out, you need a regular escape valve. I have found the following formula helpful.

- Maintain a nourishing relationship with a life partner. My wife and I divided up child-rearing duties and (now empty-nested) still divide up home-maintenance tasks as equitably as possible. Although my wife also has her doctorate and worked full-time until recently, she now prefers working at several part-time jobs, which enables her to accompany me on international professional trips.

- Avoid working in the evenings. I save that time for being with my wife and debriefing after the day's events.

- Schedule time for leisure activities, such as attending a theater production, movie, concert, or museum exhibit, or taking an overseas vacation.

- Engage in regular fitness activities. I enjoy cycling to work all year round, playing squash, and doing weight training.

- Pursue a personal interest or hobby. I play the trumpet in a community band that holds weekly rehearsals and gives concerts by the lakes in the summer.

Conclusion

We all have to find our own paths to academic achievement. I present my approaches with the recognition that they may not work for everyone. Nonetheless, I offer these generalizations based on my own experience and my observations of the work of other scholars. We must all find ways to organize our work; these will certainly be idiosyncratic, but we can learn from the organizational tactics of others. We must all find ways to live in academic systems, deciding on the roles that we take as faculty members and perhaps as administrators, and learning to make these systems work to our benefit. These are, however, external to the underlying source of academic achievement that derives from ongoing fascination with some area of study and from persistence in the pursuit of answers to our questions about that area of study. Thus, I end where I began, with content of scholarship as the essential beginning point for our journeys as scholars.

Resources

Cohen, A. D. (n.d.). *The joys of being a professor*. Retrieved February 11, 2003, from http://www1.umn.edu/ohr/teachlearn/pff/Joys/

This collection of entries is categorized by different aspects of a professor's professional work. This essentially feel-good collection demonstrates some of the ways in which the profession is joyful. The collection is also intended for those who are contemplating this type of career choice. Hard copies are available at cost from the author (by request to adcohen@umn.edu).

Cohen, A. D. (1998). *Strategies in learning and using a second language*. Harlow, England: Longman.

Cumming, A., & Swain, M. (1989). Anecdotes of accidents: Second language research going awry and telling us why. *Second Language Research, 5*(1), 74–87.

Mayer, J. J. (1995). *Time management for dummies*. Foster City, CA: IDG Books Worldwide.

Although most of what I learned about time management I got from courses on personal growth, I found this book helpful.

Parker, J., Heitzman, S., Fjerstad, A. J., Babbs, L. M., & Cohen, A. D. (1995). Exploring the role of foreign language in immersion education: Implications for SLA theory and L2 pedagogy. In F. R. Eckman, D. Highland, P. W. Lee, J. Milcham, & R. R. Weber (Eds.), *Second language acquisition theory and pedagogy* (pp. 235–253). Mahwah, NJ: Erlbaum.

University of Minnesota. (n.d.). *Andrew D. Cohen* [Personal profile]. Retrieved February 10, 2003, from http://carla.acad.umn.edu/profiles/cohen-profile.html

My personal Web site is hosted on the University of Minnesota's Center for Advanced Research on Language Acquisition Web site.

Contributor

Andrew D. Cohen (adcohen@tc.umn.edu) is in the Department of ESL at the University of Minnesota, in Minneapolis, in the United States, and directs the National Language Resource Center at the Center for Advanced Research on Language Acquisition (CARLA). In addition to articles on language learning, teaching, and assessment, he is author of *Assessing Language Ability in the Classroom* (Heinle & Heinle, 1994), coeditor with Lyle Bachman of *Interfaces Between Second*

Language Acquisition and Language Testing Research (Cambridge University Press, 1998), and coeditor with Elaine Tarone and Susan Gass of *Research Methodology in Second-Language Acquisition* (Erlbaum, 1994). He has also published books on language learning and use strategies, including *Language Learning: Insights for Learners, Teachers, and Researchers* (Newbury House/HarperCollins, 1990) and *Strategies in Learning and Using a Second Language* (Longman, 1998).

3 Outside In, Inside Out: Creating a Teaching Portfolio

Rosie Tanner

Narrative _____

One day, my colleague Ivonne and I were talking in her office when a middle-aged, balding stranger with thick-rimmed glasses walked in. With a brief handshake and a short word of congratulations, he presented me with a cream-colored "Basic University Education Qualification" certificate. The significance of the brief ceremony had not escaped Ivonne, and she clapped with enthusiasm.

"Who was *that*?" I asked, after the stranger had gone. "Oh," replied Ivonne, "that's the stand-in head of department." For a split second that feeling returned—the feeling of being an outsider, even though I had worked in the department for over a year. Nonetheless, it was a red-letter day, for during that strange, minute-long ritual, I had received my diploma for completing my portfolio and met the requirement for all new staff at Utrecht University who wish to obtain tenure.

Description

This chapter describes the creation of my educational portfolio. In the 1990s, Utrecht University implemented a new policy that required all teaching staff, as opposed to research staff, to obtain a basic qualification certificate; this change was deemed necessary in order for teaching staff to be more valued as professionals and experts in their fields. The portfolio had been mentioned during the interview before I was hired as a teacher educator. After a few short months in my post, I was confronted with the daunting fact that I had to prove myself competent for the job by compiling a portfolio illustrating my skills and knowledge. I received instructions in a handbook and a list of 45 areas in which I was to demonstrate my competency, for example, "The teacher can develop effective, efficient, activating and motivating classes, lesson and study material"; "The teacher has the social skills to be able to communicate with students and colleagues"; and "The teacher can reflect on his/her own work and can formulate alternative ways of working."

A portfolio is a selection of illustrations or evidence made by an individual, substantiated by a written reflective commentary, and created for a purpose. Educational portfolios are roughly classified as having three primary goals: evaluation, employment, and professional growth (Tanner, Longayroux, Beijaard, & Verloop, 2000; Wolf & Dietz, 1998). The portfolio I was required to create was basically an evaluation portfolio, but because of its nature, it gradually became a portrait of my own professional growth.

As an experienced teacher educator, I have worked for many years with portfolios. I have coached teacher learners in how to compile them, written guidelines and evaluation forms for them, and written articles on them (Tanner et al., 2000). I have supervised paper portfolios and, more recently, electronic portfolios. I have given workshops at conferences and advice to other faculties on the implementation of portfolios. However, I had never actually compiled one myself until I faced the requirement at Utrecht University.

Initially, I found the idea that I had to prove my skills as a teacher educator preposterous. I had had two long interviews and discussed my curriculum vita and experience at length. Were my references not enough? I had had a varied career of more than 20 years in teacher education and as a writer. Yet behind my feeling that the requirement was ludicrous were perhaps more significant feelings of uncertainty and a tinge of fear. Could I prove to my senior colleagues that I really was capable of the job?

Steps

There is no prescribed procedure for putting an educational portfolio together, although there are suggestions made in the literature (e.g., Wade & Yarbrough, 1996; Wolf, 1998; see also the Resources section). The steps depend on the purpose of your portfolio, but in any case, creating a portfolio is a dynamic process, rather like the weaving of a spider's web, with threads that connect, reconnect, and entwine at different moments along the way to form a finished product. As I developed my portfolio, I returned to earlier steps, wove new links, and reorganized. The steps below thus form loose guidelines that you can adjust according to your own context.

1. Clarify the portfolio's purpose. This step is the most important one. Be clear about why and for whom you are making your portfolio.

2. Read official guidelines. Familiarize yourself with any procedure or instructions provided for you, and examine carefully the standards or criteria by which your portfolio will be assessed. Knowing this information in advance can help you begin to collect your thoughts and illustrations and ensure that you will include all the required elements.

3. Create your portfolio over time. Making a portfolio takes time, probably several months. I did not begin to think about my portfolio early enough. I would have liked to include more student evaluations, for example, but I had read and discarded some before I became familiar enough with the regulations. Save too much rather than too little.

4. Borrow and read other people's portfolios for examples. I was encouraged to collaborate in this way and found that it helped with organization and content. In turn, new colleagues have borrowed my finished product.

5. Collect illustrations to support your teaching effectiveness. To clarify the types of illustrations to use, read about or discuss the possible illustrations, referring back to portfolios developed by colleagues. Varied types of illustrations or evidence sketch an authentic, rich, and complex picture of your teaching. Reserve a place—a box, computer file, folder, or shelf—to collect varied illustrations. Also consider which evidence best illustrates your past achievements. At this stage, start to classify your illustrations roughly, for instance, by labeling different parts of your collection by theme or area of competence.

6. Select your illustrations. At this stage, the reflection and planning process begins in earnest. Reflect on your choice of evidence: Why are you including this particular illustration, and which competencies or skills or knowledge does it show? Ideally, your illustrations should demonstrate different aspects of yourself. For example, I included a video to demonstrate my teaching competence, a list of my publications to document my writing skills, and feedback to students on their portfolios and lesson plans to illustrate my ability to assess.

7. Discuss your portfolio with colleagues, and invite a close colleague to read and comment on a draft. Most of my colleagues had already made their portfolios; a few were making one at the same time that I was. Some had done the minimum; others had done a thorough job and included fascinating illustrations and in-depth reflective comments. By receiving feedback on mine and by reading the portfolios of others, I could incorporate ideas that had not originally occurred to me and produced a more coherent and creative product.

8. Assemble your portfolio. Organize it transparently so that readers can easily follow along. For example, use colored file dividers to organize it into themes. Mull over the structure that will provide the most clarity. Write and rewrite your reflections, your philosophy of teaching, or both, depending on what is required, and ask others for feedback. Your written commentary is the spider in the web. It spins your illustrations together and

transforms a folio, which would otherwise be a random collection of illustrations, into an integrated portfolio.

9. Leave time for incubation. Make sure you have time to put your writing aside and return to it later to reread and make changes.

10. Hand in your portfolio. Without a completion date, you might be tempted to continue working on your portfolio indefinitely. I gave myself a deadline and stuck to it.

11. Follow through with your portfolio interview to complete the process. Prepare by rereading your portfolio. Be clear about the aims of the interview: Is it to decide if you will obtain tenure or to help you develop as a professional? Also, decide what you want from the interview. On reflection, I could have been much more proactive. As it was, although my interview was a pleasant, two-way experience that focused on my strengths and concluded with some important learning goals for the next year, if I should go through the process again, I wish I had prepared a few discussion questions beforehand. One question might have been: "One of my important conclusions is that, despite a lot of experience in coaching students, I still feel inadequate in some areas of coaching. Do you have any suggestions about what I might do about this?"

Conclusion

Although the requirements set by my university got me started, I learned much more than they could have possibly intended. I crystallized my skills and knowledge as a teacher educator. By turning myself inside out and reflecting on myself, I honed my skills as a portfolio coach and teacher educator, and I developed new, more coherent, stronger insights about my work, which I believe I would not have gained in such depth without having designed the portfolio. Plus, I got tenure.

Resources

Barrett, H. (n.d.). *Electronic portfolios.* Retrieved February 12, 2003, from http://electronicportfolios.com/

This site, created by Helen Barrett, in the School of Education at the University of Alaska, in Anchorage, offers information on developing an electronic portfolio.

Iowa State University, Center for Teaching Excellence. (n.d.). *ISU CTE: Teaching portfolios.* Retrieved July 3, 2002, from http://www.cte.iastate.edu/portfolio/

This site offers guidelines for making portfolios.

Lyons, N. (Ed.). (1998). *With portfolio in hand: Validating the new professionalism.* New York: Teachers College Press.

This collection of articles about teaching portfolios describes their historical development, emerging practices, the puzzles they raise, and ways to judge them.

Tanner, R., Longayroux, D., Beijaard, D., & Verloop, N. (2000). Piloting portfolios: Using portfolios in pre-service teacher education. *English Language Teaching Journal, 54*(1), 20–30.

This article gives an account of the use of portfolios for professional development in a postgraduate teacher education course.

Towson University. (n.d.). *Online teaching portfolios.* Retrieved February 12, 2003, from http://www.towson.edu/~pryan/technologyintegration/studentport.htm

This site, created by Tricia Ryan, provides examples of online portfolios.

University of Virginia, Curry School of Education. (n.d.). *Electronic teaching portfolios.* Retrieved March 21, 2002, from http://curry.edschool.virginia.edu/curry/class/edlf/589_004/sample.html

This site offers online examples of electronic portfolios made by pre- and in-service elementary and secondary school teachers, professors, and graduate students.

Wade, R. C., & Yarbrough, D. B. (1996). Portfolios: A tool for reflective thinking in teacher education? *Teaching and Teacher Education, 12*(1), 63–79.

Wolf, D. (1998). Creating a portfolio culture. In N. Lyons (Ed.), *With portfolio in hand: Validating the new professionalism* (pp. 41–50). New York: Teachers College Press.

This article explains how portfolios can contribute to a richer, more complex approach to learning for students and teachers.

Wolf, K., & Dietz, M. (1998). Teaching portfolios: Purposes and possibilities. *Teacher Education Quarterly, 25*(1), 9–22.

This article gives an overview of different types of teaching portfolios and their purposes.

Contributor _____

Rosie Tanner (rosie.tanner@wxs.nl) is a British teacher educator at the Institute of Education, at Utrecht University, in the Netherlands, where she teaches mostly language methodology in pre- and in-service programs. She is coauthor of the two-volume set, *Tasks for Teacher Education: A Reflective Approach* (Addison-Wesley Longman, 1998). Her professional interests include the use of portfolios in teacher education and applications of multiple intelligences theory to teacher and adult education.

Challenges and Motivations: Organizing a Drama Festival for High School Students

Ayşegül Daloğlu

Narrative

It was May 2000. I was thrilled to be holding the drama festival for the INGED (the acronym for *Ingilizce Egitimi Dernegi*, the Turkish name for the Association of English Language Teachers) in Ankara, Turkey. As I watched the students and their teachers entering the theater hall, I could sense their excitement. They had invested a lot of time and energy in preparing for this event. Some groups arrived with bags of costumes, some with musical instruments, and others with elaborate stage decorations. All these items demonstrated their commitment to the drama festival.

At the beginning of the festival, I had my worries about how the day would go. Would the students enjoy it? Would they take the festival seriously? What if the groups did not follow the schedule and spent too much time on stage? What if some teams did not have time to perform? After the performances started, however, I relaxed and observed how seriously the students and coaches were taking the event. The judges were watching the performances in the front row and filling in their forms. At the end of the day, the most common question was, "When is the next INGED Drama Festival?" I could see the event was a success. For nearly 20 years I had dreamed of holding such a festival, and now that dream had finally become a reality.

Description

When I started my teaching career in a high school about 20 years ago, a challenge I faced was arousing students' motivation to learn English. In Turkey, and probably in other settings where students' native language is the medium for communication, exposure to English is limited to formal instruction. Lack of exposure to the language outside the classroom and limited immediate needs for learners to use English encouraged me to create opportunities for my high school students to use English. Back then, however, I had neither the time nor the experience to structure extracurricular opportunities. Now, after completing my doctoral studies and working with preservice teachers at the university, I was able to address one of the main challenges of my first year in teaching by fostering activities to increase students' motivation. The idea of organizing a drama festival was attractive for several reasons. First, I had been working at the university level for a long time and was beginning to forget the realities of teaching in high school, where most of the student teachers I instructed worked after completing their studies. I therefore needed to get in touch with their reality.

Second, organizing a drama festival would provide me with a new challenge and variety. After teaching the same courses in the same university for a few years, I needed a refreshing change.

Third, the festival could give students an authentic reason to practice and use English. It could also encourage them to develop a positive attitude toward the language, the culture associated with the language, and language learning.

Finally, making this festival one of the events of INGED would serve a wider community. Not only would it benefit the students and teachers directly involved, it would also provide a service to the association as well.

The task of organizing the INGED Drama Festival was a yearlong process that started with contacting the different parties that would be involved. First, in October, I contacted the English departments of high schools that provide English language courses to inquire if they would be interested in participating in such a festival. The positive response and enthusiasm of the schools motivated me to pursue the idea.

Next, I asked the teachers in the interested schools to nominate one teacher from each of their schools to coach their students for the festival as well as attend preparation meetings with the other coaches. Only high schools in Ankara were invited to the festival because the coaches had to be able to attend meetings easily, and arranging accommodations for the participating students would have been costly and difficult.

Eight coaches and I formed the festival planning team. As the festival coordinator and the liaison with the different parties involved, I had three roles:

1. communicator with the high schools and the coaching teachers: I invited the coaches to regular meetings, at first with the aim of establishing the purposes of the festival. Later, we discussed methods and techniques that could foster a positive attitude toward English and learning English. Finding the appropriate place to hold meetings was challenging because the coaches worked and lived in different parts of Ankara. We chose the British Council as our meeting site.

2. communicator with the sponsors: The sponsors of the festival were publishers, the Public Affairs Section of the U.S. Embassy, the British Council, and a high school. The contributions of these sponsors ranged from providing the venue to providing financial support that covered the lunch and awards.

3. communicator with the judges: Three judges who were active English language teaching professionals evaluated the performances of all the teams at the festival based on predetermined criteria. I met with the judges in advance to establish the assessment criteria so that the coaching teachers could be apprised of them before the festival. At the first meeting, the festival date was set for May to give the schools sufficient time to choose or script a play and to prepare a stage production of it.

Once the number of participating schools was established (there were eight), we, the festival planning team, focused on the operational aspects of the festival. First, we calculated the amount of stage time each school could have, given the fact that the festival was a 1-day event. Also, after the venue was identified, we figured out how many students each school could bring as its audience, based on the size of the theater hall and the cafeteria, which had to accommodate all the coaches, performers, and audience members during the same 40-minute lunch break.

After reaching a consensus on the logistical details of the festival, the planning team focused on the types of performances that could be staged. Our main aim was to identify a framework that was flexible enough to foster creativity but structured enough to reach the aims of the festival. As a result, we decided not to impose restrictions on the types of performances. Teams could choose a storytelling activity, a play, a duet, or a combination of these three, provided that they did not exceed the amount of stage time allocated to each school (20 minutes). Some teams chose a comedy while others preferred a classic tragedy, such as *Romeo and Juliet*. Some wrote their own scripts while others adapted plays they had studied in their courses.

In regularly scheduled meetings during the academic year, coaches shared the pieces their groups were working on and the activities they were using to make students more aware of the linguistic features and acting techniques for their performances. Specifically, we focused on activities that would engage students in all four skill areas: reading, writing, speaking, and listening. For instance, we had students read plays and stories and share them with their team members in the process of choosing one to be staged. We also had students work in groups to write and practice pronunciation (especially intonation and stress patterns). Although some teams chose to include music and even composed it themselves, we discouraged them from using too much music and dance because this would limit the amount of language practice they would get from the experience.

At the meetings, we also discussed the extent to which this event was a festival or a competition. The members of the planning team agreed that having an awards ceremony to acknowledge students' efforts would motivate students and coaching teachers to participate in the following years. At that stage, I emphasized the importance of creating a festival atmosphere that would foster sharing and having fun as well as encourage each group to display its best stage performance. Coaches, perhaps due to student pressure, were at times inclined to view the event as a competition rather than a festival. We tried to overcome this by emphasizing that the main aim of the festival was to develop a positive attitude in students toward learning English. As an incentive, each performer received a certificate of participation at the end of the festival. In addition, the judges awarded three trophies in each of eight categories for Best Actor, Best Actress, Most Promising Actor, Most Promising Actress, Best Costume, Best Play, Best Music, and Best Visual Effects. After the festival, the students said they enjoyed the awards ceremony immensely because it resembled the Academy Awards, a ceremony hosted annually in the United States in recognition of outstanding achievements in film.

Steps

Below are several suggestions for planning a successful festival.

1. Establish a forum of communication among coaches working at different schools. Communication is especially important to ensure that all coaches and students feel they have a chance to express their opinions, which directly affects their ownership of decisions. In addition, this forum serves to identify the training needs of the coaches and enables you to hold miniworkshops directly related to the coaches' current tasks. If coaches feel left out of the communication network, they might perceive that other schools have an advantage in the competition.

2. Allow sufficient time to prepare for the festival. The festival is only a 1-day event, but most of the learning and development take place during the preparation for it. The feedback forms that the coaches submitted at the festival demonstrated that they believed they had improved their teaching and management skills in the preparation process. On their feedback forms, performers emphasized that they had improved their language knowledge and skills, especially pronunciation (stress and intonation) and vocabulary, when searching for and rehearsing a production piece.

3. Acknowledge the time and effort the coaches and students invest in the festival in the form of a certificate, award, or verbal expression of thanks at the awards ceremony. Because the coaches and students do nearly all of the preparation outside of school hours and mostly on weekends, the festival is an outcome of their dedication. Acknowledgment of their efforts improves their self-confidence, commitment to such extracurricular activities, and motivation to teach and learn. When I visited some of the participating schools following the festival, I saw that the coaches had displayed their certificates on their office walls.

Conclusion

As mentioned, the feedback from the coaches and participating teachers demonstrated that they had benefited from the experience. More specifically, the coaches felt more confident as teachers, especially when providing students with language practice activities and communicating with their colleagues. Several coaches described how some students who had performed poorly on class assignments displayed enthusiasm for the festival and made an effort to develop their language skills. In addition, most coaches reported feeling better equipped with language teaching strategies that prepare students for such an event. Moreover, the fact that all coaches requested that the festival become an annual INGED event indicates its impact.

Organizing this festival contributed to my professional development in numerous ways. It gave me a chance to reacquaint myself with teaching English in high schools. Although I started my teaching career at the high school level and now instruct student teachers who will work at that level, I realized I was more isolated than I thought from the actual context. At times, I was shocked to see that I had forgotten the characteristics and demands of such learners. Organizing this festival refreshed my memory on what teaching high school students is like and what the needs of such teachers and learners are.

In preparing and delivering the workshops for the coaches, I improved my knowledge of and skills in coaching students for a festival. Before the festival, my main path to self-development had been delivering presentations at national and international conferences. The festival provided me with a specific focus on which to improve myself professionally.

Most important, organizing the festival added variety and liveliness to my professional life, which had become rather monotonous. Although it was demanding, the festival was well worth the time and energy invested. When I look back, the main source of fulfillment was observing the students' enjoyment and the coaches' pride while watching the students perform on stage. The festival has become an annual INGED event.

Resources

Cramer, D. (1996). *Motivating high level learners*. Essex, England: Longman.

This book identifies strategies and techniques to promote student involvement. It provides insights on how and why students undertake challenges and how teachers or coaches can motivate them.

Erion, P., & Lewis, J. C. (1996). *Drama in the classroom: Creative activities for teachers, parents, and friends*. Fort Bragg, CA: Lost Coast Press.

McCaslin, N. (1999). *Creative drama in the classroom and beyond*. New York: Longman.

These sources provide guidelines for using drama activities in the classroom.

Contributor

Ayşegül Daloğlu (aygul@fedu.metu.edu.tr) is an assistant professor in the Department of Foreign Language Education at the Middle East Technical University, in Ankara, Turkey. Her areas of professional interest include curriculum and materials design and evaluation, teacher development, and assessment in English language teaching. She is a founding member of INGED, the Association of English Language Teachers in Turkey, and a member of the TESOL board of directors.

5 Writing for Grant Dollar$

Jane E. Averill

Narrative

It was March 1989, just a year after I had been appointed director of a small intensive English program at Emporia State University, in Emporia, Kansas, in the United States. To do this job, I wanted more training in intercultural communications so that I could work more effectively with students and better understand other regions of the world.

Then, one day, I noticed information about structured individual training grants in a newsletter published by NAFSA: Association of International Educators. I completed the grant application, got letters of support from administrators, and approximately 3 months later, received a letter stating that I had received a grant of $400 to defray transportation costs to attend the Summer Institute for Intercultural Communication in Portland, Oregon. That $400 does not sound like much these days, but it made a huge difference to me at the time. In addition to receiving the training, that original grant got me started down the grant-writing road.

These days, however, I am more likely to be working on grants for $400,000 than for $400. I am also likely to be working with several others rather than alone. On a recent government grant, several colleagues and I spent about 4 weeks writing and rewriting our idea to use our expertise in instructional technology with a teacher education program. Instead of the single copy I submitted for the NAFSA grant, we were dealing with multiple copies of a complex document. As with the small grant, we had a waiting period. Approximately 5 months later, we finally received a letter. Shouts of joy filled the hall. These successes do not come easily or even often, but when they do, they make the whole process worthwhile.

Description

In these days of shrinking budgets and the do-more-with-less administrative model, ESL educators from elementary schools to universities are finding that they need to seek new revenue sources. Thinking about writing a grant can be intimidating, but if you have a compelling idea that you communicate with good writing skills, measurable objectives, and a realistic budget, you can create opportunities that would otherwise not exist for your school or your students.

I once heard someone refer to grant writing as similar to childbirth. That may be a good metaphor for the successful grant, considering the intensity of the experience and the temporary discomfort it can cause. After giving birth to the document, there is a sense of deep relief and exhaustion coupled with satisfaction. The proposal then takes on a life of its own, as you either receive funding and move into a management stage or revise with new input and resubmit. Writing and revising a grant is seldom boring and, like parenthood, produces a great sense of pride, accomplishment, and personal growth as you realize how you have helped lead the process.

Do not be discouraged if your grant is not funded the first time you submit it. According to *In Search of Funding* (Wallen, 1990), four out of five grant applications are rejected, and the competition is becoming increasingly fierce. If you have a good idea, however, persist and make sure you communicate to the right people or agency how your idea will make a difference. ESL teachers have one huge advantage in the grant-writing game: Most are well trained in how to communicate effectively through the written word. Grant-writing workshops offered on many college campuses and books on the process focus a good deal of attention on the need for an effective narrative. Therefore, a trained writer has an advantage.

In deciding if writing a grant is a good solution for your situation, you will definitely need the support of your administrators, other participants in the grant, and even your family. You will most likely need to write the grant in addition to everything else you do, so expect to sacrifice some of your free time for a while. Also solicit the help of someone to be your editor and a member of your support team. To calculate how much time a grant will take to write, some sources recommend taking the time you think it will take and adding at least 2 weeks. This, of course, depends on the complexity of the grant.

Steps _____

Preparing for Opportunities

1. Examine your personal and institutional capabilities. If you are thinking about writing grants, figure out your own strengths and those of your institution. Know what kinds of projects you personally, or as part of an institution, could do creatively. Grants do not supply funds to continue business as usual, so find a new angle.

2. Develop your skills. I gained insights into the reviewing process and the importance of following the guidelines in a request for proposal (RFP) by reading grants for the Office of Bilingual Education and Minority Language Affairs. Local organizations may offer similar opportunities. If an organization offers small start-up grants or requires application procedures, you may be able to volunteer to help in the process. Although books and the Internet can provide you with most of the nuts and bolts of grant writing, I prefer attending the workshops offered by the research office at Oregon State University (OSU), where I work. These workshops have given me ideas on everything from budgets to institutional requirements and have put me in touch with successful grant writers who served as mentors.

3. Start small. Is there a project that you can do for several hundred dollars? It is easier to find an organization that offers small grants. Check local resources. If your idea involves the community, there may be local companies that provide start-up funds for the right idea.

4. Subscribe to e-mail lists that provide regular information on funding opportunities. This will enable you to easily review opportunities listed in sources, such as the *Federal Register*, published by the U.S. Government Printing Office.

Getting Down to Business

There are basically two ways to approach grant writing: (a) responding to an RFP and (b) writing an unsolicited proposal, meaning you have to sell your idea to agencies that fund the kind of activity you want to do.

5. Once you find an RFP that interests you, check the requirements. Ask yourself a series of important questions, for example, Do you and your institution have the expertise to meet the objectives of the RFP? Do you have the time? Can you involve others who bring additional knowledge and skills to the project?

6. Do your homework thoroughly. If you plan to submit an unsolicited proposal to a foundation or a development office, research the funders that are most likely to be interested in your project. Try to find a match between the goals and objectives of your project and those of the funders. It is often a good idea to call a potential funder before you submit to make sure your proposal fits the goals of the foundation. If you are responding to an RFP, follow the format and requirements of the proposal request very carefully. Pay attention to deadlines, formatting requirements, supporting documentation, and length. Clarify any questions with the project officer well before the deadline.

7. Obtain firm commitments from people who will be involved in the grant. A strong team of key personnel with the right qualifications will go a long way in convincing the funder of your ability to complete the project successfully. It is helpful to

have a set of current résumés on hand to find the best match in project personnel.

8. Create a time line that works backward from your deadline. Include time to write several drafts, receive feedback from others, gather the materials you need to submit, and research and prepare the budget. At OSU, we must submit grant proposals to our research office as the final step before submitting the grant to the funder. The research office checks the budget and gives an institutional stamp of approval. This process takes at least several days. Make sure you allow enough time for revisions that may be requested.

Writing the Proposal

9. Follow the organization outlined in the RFP. Most proposals include a narrative, a budget, and appendixes as well as items such as curricula vitae, time lines, letters of cooperation, and certifications and other requirements requested by the funder.

10. Create a thorough narrative. Introduce your institution or organization, and explain the need for your project. Outline your capacity for carrying out the project in terms of experience, personnel, evaluation plan, and resources. State clear objectives, and align them with the funder's goals. Explain in detail how the project will work and how it will be implemented and evaluated.

11. Do not be intimidated by the word *budget*. I always find that the budget is a way to help me review what I have written and figure out the details of how it will work. If I say, for example, that we will offer a small computer course in a traveling lab, I need to consider how many laptop computers to purchase or decide if I should rent a lab in a school. Other questions come to mind: Whom will I have to hire to handle the technical aspects (e.g., checking Internet connections, networking computers, troubleshooting problems)? How much will it cost to travel to the location? Plan expenditures realistically and think about details, including how many hours a task (e.g., loading software) will take. Keep in mind that budgets are

planning documents. Include contingencies for unexpected expenses, but guess at costs as accurately as possible. Funders will look at this section very carefully, so think of ways to demonstrate that you will use their money wisely. If your budget is too lean, funders may wonder if you can do the job adequately. If it is too generous, they will look for another proposal. They may want to negotiate the cost at some point, so be prepared for some compromise.

Putting on the Finishing Touches

12. Make sure you submit a neat, clear proposal on time. Pay attention to all the requirements so that your hard work is not disqualified. Make sure you have included all the necessary parts in all of the copies. Look for a checklist included in the RFP, or develop your own.

13. Wait for the results. You should hear by the date specified, but you may check the status of your submission by telephone after a reasonable amount of time. After sending the proposal, recognize the efforts of everyone involved in the writing. Remember, completing the process is itself an accomplishment.

14. Follow up after the proposal is evaluated. Sometimes you can get useful information about the proposal if it is rejected. One project officer recommended other funding sources that might be interested and suggested ways to strengthen my proposal.

Conclusion

My professional experiences in TESOL have been almost as diverse as the students I have taught. When I began teaching more than 25 years ago, I never imagined that my degree would lead me into calculating budgets for grants or helping raise more than a million dollars in grants and contracts in a year. My current position requires me to have an entrepreneurial spirit, develop new programs, and keep the bottom line in mind. I know that diversifying income sources at the English Language Institute at OSU has helped us weather the decline in enrollment following the recent downturns in the Asian economic sector and the tragedies of the terrorist plane crashes in the United States on September 11, 2001. Personally, I find excitement in the endless creativity that grant writing offers. I can mold the ideal program and figure out how to make it work within a realistic context. I also enjoy the camaraderie generated by collaborating within a tight time frame to achieve a group goal. When a grant I have written is selected for funding, it is like winning a game show or watching my child become a star performer. Most importantly, the grants helped create opportunities we could not have provided otherwise. In 2001, we were fortunate to have received three large grants that helped us work with groups of public school teachers in Oregon and outside the United States.

I still credit that first $400 grant for having given me the courage to start writing grants, and I credit my current supervisor for having guided me further with a productive, team-oriented atmosphere that values creativity. Many opportunities await you, too, if you decide to write for dollar$.

Resources

Brewer, E. W., Achilles, C. M., Fuhriman, J. R., & Hollingsworth, C. (2001). *Finding funding* (4th ed.). Thousand Oaks, CA: Corwin.

This book offers a step-by-step process for grant writing, tips on project management, and a sample grant.

Corporation for Public Broadcasting. (2002). *Basic elements of grant writing*. Retrieved February 20, 2002, from http://www.cpb.org/grants/grantwriting.html

This site contains interesting information on what a funder might look for, especially a nonprofit, educational organization.

Wallen, D. (Creator), & Walsh, L. (Writer). (1990). *In search of funding* [Video]. (Available from the Office of Research Services, University of New Mexico, Albuquerque, NM 87131-6003)

Wallen, D. (Creator), & Walsh, L. (Writer). (n.d.). *In search of funding*. Retrieved March 5, 2003, from http://www.unm.edu/~ors/publications/I_S_O_F.html

Much of the information on the video is available here.

Contributor

Jane E. Averill (jane.averill@orst.edu) is the coordinator of Special Programs at the English Language Institute at Oregon State University, in the United States. She has worked as an ESL administrator and teacher since 1978 in university, community college, and K–12 settings in the United States, Brazil, and Japan.

6 The Roller Coaster Ride of Editing a Book

John M. Murphy

Narrative

It was a peaceful afternoon in May, and the work was intensive. For several weeks, manuscripts had been arriving in the mail. Rather than dedicating myself to my own efforts as a writer, I was devoting more and more time to thinking over and editing other writers' prose. Although I was getting up earlier each morning and struggling with many of the manuscripts before me, the funny thing was that I was enjoying myself. One of my sisters phoned that afternoon while I was sitting in a lounge chair, pen in hand, with a pile of manuscripts at my side. After catching up on recent family events, I remember hearing myself say, "You know, I want to spend all of my months of May this way." I had reached a point in the book project that I can only describe as thrilling.

A large part of my excitement was due to the fact that I had enticed a group of specialists whose work I knew and respected to compose manuscripts for book chapters based on a conceptual scheme of my own design. Now that the manuscripts were arriving, I found myself in the fortunate position of being able to enjoy, assess, argue with, and comment on the substance of the other contributors' work. I know that my reactions to their draft manuscripts covered a wide range of emotions. My son had a baseball game that weekend, and it was all I could do to force myself to leave the manuscripts. Happily, the game was exciting, too, but I have to admit that during its slower phases—especially while other fathers' sons were at bat—my mind drifted to the work waiting for me at home.

As might be expected, not all the stages of the book project were this satisfying. At times I was unsure if I would ever be able to interest others in the concept for the book. There were periods of self-doubt and confusion when I thought my efforts would be in vain. I made the rounds of several publishing houses before finding the right home for the book. There was a period of temporary security once I found an acquisitions editor with whom I was comfortable working and who showed genuine enthusiasm for the project. After we had developed a good working relationship, however, I was thrown into a tailspin one afternoon when a brief e-mail message informed me that she was moving to another publishing house. Her assurances that her replacement would be just as helpful did little to assuage my concerns. For several days I worried if the 18 months I had already put into the project might be wasted. Happily, my fears were unfounded.

At another stage in the project, the publisher arranged for outside reviewers to comment on the quality and potential of early drafts of several chapters. I recognized that their recommendations would involve considerable work and would extend the time line I had developed. As I examined what they had in mind, my blood pressure increased, my palms got sweaty, and I whispered something like a prayer for the strength to survive the amount of work the changes would involve. As most writers will recognize, such emotional responses are inevitable parts of the process. Though we may feel overwhelmed at first, writer-editors discover some central strengths while working on book projects, including patience, the ability to focus energies and thoughts, and creativity in applying abilities as a writer and thinker to seemingly insurmountable tasks. Editing a book includes extended periods of calm, peaceful work of great substance straddled by brief roller coaster rides when the entire project seems to be leaping out of one's control. Looking back on the process, the roller coaster rides seem less traumatic. My memories of the periods of peaceful work remind me of how much I enjoyed and benefited from the project.

Description

The role of a book editor is quite different from what I expected. It begins with an idea or vision for a professional publication that you have an interest in but for which limited resources are available. In my case, I had been teaching an MA TESOL methods course twice a year for more than a decade when I began to feel that I could make a contribution to it. I knew the literature on second language (L2) teaching methods and on ways of offering methods courses, but I had quite a few dissatisfactions and concerns. From this experience, I learned that knowing the literature for the targeted content area extremely well is essential to serving as a book editor.

Book editors need to have a vision and be able to convince others that the vision is important for the future of the field. This effort carries tremendous responsibility because the book's contributors will be devoting considerable time and energy to working on manuscripts that will have to align with the editor's vision. I decided to become an editor for a book because I had a clear idea that seemed important, and I knew that I would need to collaborate with other writers to bring the idea to fruition.

What does it take to be a book editor? How does one find the right vision? When is the right time to reach out and try to interest others in your vision? I suspect that these questions have many answers. The steps I describe below grew out of some of the lessons I learned while involved in my own book project (Murphy & Byrd, 2001). What follows, though, is more than a retrospective description of the steps my colleague and I followed. The steps below include additional ones we realized as a result of having participated in the book-editing process.

1. Know your area of specialization. There really is no substitute for knowing your area well. Read widely in the available literature. Contribute to the literature by establishing a track record of journal publications. You need to become known by others as someone whose ideas are worthy of attention and valued in the field. In my case, two journal articles from early stages of my career served as illustrations for the kinds of book chapters I asked other contributors to compose.

2. Stay true to your own interest and passions. Find an area in your professional life that really sparks your interest. To have the energy, enthusiasm, and stamina to organize and edit an entire book, you must have a topic that will carry you through good times and bad.

3. Consult others. Take the time to talk in depth with someone you trust who has written or edited a book. How did they find their topics? How much time did their project take? How did they locate contributors and a publisher?

4. Put your idea(s) in writing. Try setting forth the basic idea for the book in 250–500 words that will be accessible to a nonspecialist as you prepare to convince an acquisitions editor of the value of your idea. Though some acquisitions editors may have background in language teaching, do not assume they are as knowledgeable as you about current trends in the research and teaching ofL2s. They are the kinds of readers you will have to sell your idea to if the book project is to go forward.

5. Create an Internet site. Once I had a firm idea of what I wanted the book to include, I created an Internet site outlining what I had in mind. Once the site was posted on the Web, sharing the site's address with specialists in the field who were possible contributors to the book was simple.

6. Compose a prospectus. Part of the process of attracting attention to a book project is submitting a prospectus to an acquisitions editor. Read and study a guide to developing a prospectus (e.g., *Material Writer's Guide*, Byrd, 1995) for the

practical information presented and for a realistic portrayal of the publication process. Focus on the sections most relevant to the kind of book you have in mind. The content and format of a prospectus for an ESL classroom textbook, a single-authored book, or an edited collection differ in significant and subtle ways.

7. Conduct a market analysis. A central component of the prospectus will be your description and review of books already available in the professional literature that will be competing with your book once it is published. You need to know your competition well in order to convince others that your contribution to the literature will be marketable and worthwhile.

8. Shop your idea around. A book prospectus is different from a manuscript being prepared for submission as a journal article. It is accepted practice to submit a prospectus to multiple publishers for consideration. Of course, you need to maintain professional integrity. If you show a prospectus to different publishers, inform all of them that they are not the only ones reviewing it.

9. Create a manageable time line. Think in terms of how much time you will need to complete the various stages of your project. When do you want the book to be available? During which periods of the year do you have time for the labor-intensive work of editing? For example, I structured the time line for my project so that contributors could complete most of their work on an initial draft during May through August (1998). I read and provided feedback on their initial drafts during September through October. Contributors revised the initial drafts based on my feedback from November through February. This time line afforded me the period of March through May (1999) to finalize my work on individual chapters while still exchanging drafts and revisions with some contributors.

10. Stay in close contact with contributors. The quality of an edited collection depends on how successful you are in getting other writers to share your vision for the book. Unless you are

working with local colleagues with whom face-to-face meetings are possible, e-mail exchanges are likely to be your primary means for staying in contact.

11. Learn to keep track of online edits during draft revisions. I work in Microsoft Word, which has a "Track Changes" feature that permits you to interact with contributors throughout the editing process. You can use this feature to make suggestions, ask questions, and keep track of changes or queries to authors within the body of a manuscript. You can also display changes or insertions in a different color on the computer screen. The different colors make it easy to see the contributor's original text and to keep track of an editor's contributions, questions, or other concerns.

12. Anticipate complications, and be flexible when things go awry. A process as complex as composing and editing a book for publication is filled with potential complications. All parties involved will place countless expectations on you. Learn to anticipate such complications while developing the personal resources to deal with them.

Conclusion

Professionally and personally, writing or editing a book is extremely rewarding. Using your edited book after it has been published, and finding that others are using it, can be gratifying. At a recent TESOL convention, I was invited to conduct a publisher's presentation about the book. While winding down my presentation on how to use the book in a methods course, one of my personal heroes in the field (a well-known specialist who had delivered a plenary address at the convention earlier that afternoon) stood up, thanked me for the book, and explained that he had been using it for the past several months. He went on to say how much he and the graduate students enjoyed working with it. Needless to say, I was thrilled. Though I may initially have been apprehensive about serving as a book editor, moments like that one continue to remind me that the roller coaster ride is well worth the effort.

Resources

Byrd, P. (Ed.). (1995). *Material writer's guide*. Boston: Heinle & Heinle.

This volume provides information about the entire process of preparing a book for publication. The chapter on how to compose a book prospectus and what to do with the prospectus once completed is especially helpful.

Georgia State University. (n.d.). *Initial letter for possible contributors to a proposed text titled, "Particular approaches: Local perspectives on English language instruction."* Retrieved January 10, 2002, from http://www.gsu.edu/~esljmm/methods/initlet.htm

This is the initial site I used to introduce my book project to potential contributors.

Georgia State University. (n.d.). *Understanding the courses we teach*. Retrieved January 10, 2003, from http://www.gsu.edu/~wwwesl/understanding/

This site shows how an Internet site may be used to support a published book.

Murphy, J. M., & Byrd, H. P. (Eds.). (2001). *Understanding the courses we teach: Local perspectives on English language teaching*. Ann Arbor: University of Michigan Press.

This volume on teacher development was the result of the book project mentioned in this chapter.

Contributor

John M. Murphy (jmmurphy@gsu.edu) prepares ESL/EFL teachers in the MA and PhD programs of the Department of Applied Linguistics and ESL at Georgia State University in Atlanta, in the United States.

7 Small Corrections: Becoming a Textbook Writer

Linda Grant

Narrative _____

Spring 1982, Atlanta, Georgia. Dogwood trees are in full bloom. Rushing across the Georgia Tech campus to meet my class, I pause long enough to appreciate the good fortune that helped me land this position. A refugee from audiology, I have been teaching ESL for 3 years. I relish being on a wooded campus with some architectural character rather than in a generic, boxy office building. Mostly I appreciate the academic calendar, with new quarters, new classes, and new students with different language and cultural backgrounds. Change sets the blood coursing through my veins. If I am to be a slave to someone else's rhythms, let them be the rhythms of the academy, not a work year with only one beginning and end. That would be like living in a climate with no seasons, no color, no variety. I will need this constant change, I think.

The year is 1990, 8 years, 32 quarters, 125 classes, and 2,000 students later. Spring again, but the bloom is off the rose, or dogwood, as it were. The blood is no longer coursing. I am attending a local ESL conference at a nearby college. Attempting to rekindle the flame, I have become a conference groupie, but that provides only temporary relief. Though I still love the classroom, the daily routine is taking its toll. The itch is back. It must be time to apply for a PhD program—for the third time—or move to Maine and open that bed-and-breakfast. My mother was right; I am a malcontent, never satisfied. My husband, consistent with his training as a pilot, advises "small corrections."

Little did I know that the seed for my correction was planted that day at that conference. A well-connected colleague who knew I aspired to write an ESL pronunciation textbook introduced me to a publishing company representative (rep). That brief chat set in motion a series of events that would ultimately alter my fundamental activity in ESL from teaching to writing—a shift that has given me a new perspective of the field, provided a creative challenge, opened doors to teacher education and consulting, and kept me connected to the profession that I entered more than 20 years ago.

Description

Three weeks after the conference, much to my surprise, an acquisitions editor from Newbury House called me at home. The sales rep had pitched my idea to her, and she wanted a prospectus (a description of the project and two sample chapters), which I sent. The feedback from the editors and anonymous reviewers was favorable, and I signed a contract to write an advanced-level pronunciation text.

One year after signing the contract, the completed manuscript was sent out for another round of reviews. Based on those reviews, I made adjustments, and the text went into production. The entire cycle, from signing the contract to holding the first copy in my hand, lasted about 2 years. Within a few years of publication, the text became a best-seller, again to my surprise—and to that of my publisher. Eight years after the first edition was published, I wrote a second edition. At this writing, I am preparing a prospectus for a lower level companion to the existing text.

Although I have nurtured an interest in writing off and on since childhood, authoring textbooks did not appear on my radar screen until I had been teaching ESL for 10 years. During that time, I taught many courses in my primary area of interest and developed an expertise. I became intimate with texts and their potential to effectively instruct as well as creatively engage. Well-conceived texts made my life unquestionably easier. Texts that failed to match my teaching needs made life harder, but they also prompted me to develop the supplemental materials that became the bedrock of my text. Only in hindsight is it clear that the years teaching in an intensive English program laid this foundation. There may be many paths to successful textbook writing and maybe even some shortcuts, but few routes bypass the ESL/EFL classroom.

Steps

The nuts and bolts of ESL textbook writing vary according to your publisher. Most publishers give potential authors written guidelines for submitting a prospectus. If a contract is signed, the publisher supplies guidelines for preparing a manuscript. For general advice for would-be writers, see the Resources section.

Beyond that, I cannot offer a blueprint for shifting your professional focus to textbook writing. Some authors integrate writing with full-time work; others cannot or choose not to. About a year ago, I decided that I was not willing to juggle my full-time duties as a teacher and administrator with those of a writer, so I resigned from my position as assistant director of ESL at Emory University. That decision involved trade-offs—financial security and benefits for more time and balance—and I am still trying to manage the repercussions.

In light of my experience, I offer the following suggestions as considerations, not as a set of prescribed steps, for those contemplating the life of a writer.

1. Do not quit your day job yet. Unless you are independently wealthy, you will write your first book(s) in the context of full-time employment. That means writing in the wee hours of the morning, during vacations, and on weekends. It is the rare workplace that will accommodate your writing schedule. After all, you were hired to teach. Do not expect the equivalent of a full-time income from writing until you have several widely used texts in circulation. Even then, you will probably need to

supplement your royalty income with part-time teaching and consulting.

2. Know how and when to turn "it" off. Most would-be writers are advised to set aside time each day to think and write. Equally important is setting aside time not to think and write. If you write at home, life and work become inextricably tangled. Segmenting the two is challenging, so try to specify times and places you will and will not write. Keep notebooks handy, though. Even with rigorous writing schedules, you may get your best idea while careening down the highway at 70 mph.

3. Stay connected with colleagues. You may bid the world of full-time employment good-bye, but do not abandon your former colleagues. Writing is a solitary endeavor and a lonely business, so maintain your professional contacts (e.g., as a consultant or volunteer member of a TESOL affiliate or interest section). Over the years, the most rewarding opportunities have come to me via valued colleagues. Now that I am no longer a full-time employee of an institution, these relationships are even more important. You may also want to call on former colleagues to pilot your materials in their classrooms. What seems perfectly clear to you as a writer may not be as transparent to the user. In exchange for honest feedback, cook a great meal for those who piloted your materials.

4. Keep one foot in the ESL classroom. Love of teaching and contact with international students was why many of us entered this field in the first place. It is unfortunate to be faced with choices such as teaching full time or not at all. Moreover, it is apparent when an author has not spent time in the classroom or has taken a permanent hiatus from teaching. Although you will probably be paid a pittance for teaching as a part-timer, it is important to step back into the classroom now and then.

5. Stay in touch with novice teachers, teacher trainees, and graduate students. Senior members of the profession need to be in tune with the concerns and interests of the new generation of teachers. After all, they are the people who choose the texts. You can maintain this connection through teacher education,

networking, presenting at conferences, and attending conference presentations.

6. Keep current with theory. In the midst of a writing project, it is easy to get mired in details (e.g., direction lines, choice of vocabulary) and lose the view of the forest for the trees. Stepping back from the writing for a few days and rereading theory related to education, second language acquisition, and your area of special interest, for instance, may help clarify your thinking and set you back on the right track.

7. Maintain cordial relationships with your editors, but do not get too attached. Chances are that editors will change at least once, maybe twice, during a project. Sometimes the publisher will change, too. Keep a paper trail of all correspondence and agreements. If you want to work with the same publisher again, honor deadlines. Editors and production staff prefer to work with authors who are organized and respect timetables.

8. Choose subsequent projects carefully. If your first book is successful, doors will open. Your current publisher or other publishers may approach you with specific writing projects in mind. In such cases, you may not drive the projects and may spend more time in the passenger seat. Rather than filling a niche, these projects may compete with existing titles offered by other publishers. Ask yourself if such distinctions matter to you. Instead of single-authored volumes, new projects may involve major collaborative efforts that entail coordination with other writers. As such, these projects can be professionally and personally enriching. Finally, a publisher may ask you to serve in an advisory capacity on a project, in which case you would not write but would provide feedback to other writers.

9. Keep your relationship with your books clean. Be clear when you are representing your book and publisher and promoting your materials versus when you are sharing information in a professional presentation. Do not mix up the two.

10. Adjust your perspective on income. When you shift from full-time teaching to writing, royalties cease being discretionary and become your primary income. Your income from consulting

and part-time teaching may be minimal and unpredictable. At the same time, your expenses will probably increase as you absorb costs such as health insurance and professional development. Keep careful records for financial and professional purposes.

Conclusion

I intend to spend this summer embarking on a new writing project. Each morning I will put on my sweatpants and slippers and make the 3-second commute to my home office. I will sit at my computer searching the woods outside my office for inspiration. I may lug my laptop to the beach and wait for the muse to descend while overlooking one of my favorite stretches of the Atlantic coast. It is tough work, but somebody has to do it.

In fairness, I should point out that I will not get paid a dime during this part of the process. I should also mention that writing is excruciatingly hard work. When weighing the pros and cons of a professional life in which writing is central, test the waters and weigh major decisions carefully. The trade-offs will be different for everyone.

Resources

Byrd, P. (Ed.). (1995). *Material writer's guide*. Boston: Heinle & Heinle.

A valuable resource for ESL materials writers, this book covers a broad range of issues, from the nuts and bolts of writing and publishing to writing texts for specific types of courses, including grammar, writing, listening, pronunciation, and English for specific purposes.

Lamott, A. (1994). *Bird by bird: Some instructions on writing and life.* New York: Anchor Books.

This book presents a writer's humorous, realistic, and honest account of the ups and downs of writing, including words of wisdom, advice, and encouragement applicable to writers of fiction and textbooks alike.

TESOL. http://www.tesol.org

> From TESOL's home page, click on Communities, then follow the links to the Materials Writers Interest Section page. For TESOL members who are published writers and would-be writers, this site provides a forum for networking and sharing concerns about writing and publishing.

Contributor

Linda Grant (lgrant@hsrd.emory.edu) has taught in the intensive English program at the Georgia Institute of Technology, served as assistant director of ESL at Emory University, and taught in the Department of Applied Linguistics and ESL at Georgia State University, in the United States. The author of *Well Said: Pronunciation for Clear Communication* (2nd ed., Heinle & Heinle, 2001), she writes, consults, and educates teachers.

8 Going for the Gold: Managing an Academic Department

Siti Hamin Stapa

Narrative

When I started working as an English language instructor at the National University of Malaysia, in 1986, I never dreamed of becoming an administrator. All I was interested in was teaching English and motivating students to learn English. Then, one day in 1997, the dean of the faculty called me to her office for a meeting. When I entered her office, she asked me to sit down and then explained that the head of the Foreign Language Studies Department was leaving. She had to find a replacement and felt that I was the best candidate. I was given some time to think it over. I spent a few sleepless nights considering the offer and decided to accept it. I served as the head of the department for about $4^1/_2$ years until it merged with three others.

Description

A department head must develop a vision of excellence beyond the immediate tasks of running the department and employ strategies that develop the faculty's

59

commitment to that vision. To achieve the vision, the head must make sure to keep things simple. The head must respond to the students and the faculty, listen to the teachers and treat them as adults, and allow teachers time to analyze and innovate. Institutions of higher education require leadership to be shared more than in most profit-focused enterprises. The concept of faculty ownership is basic to academic institutions; thus, departmental leadership requires a greater emphasis on empowering activities than in many other types of organizations. In managing an academic department, you cannot just open a book on business management and use the principles as the guide. What you can do is adapt some of the principles suitable to your institution.

Steps

When I was appointed department head by the vice chancellor, I spent a few days thinking about how I could best serve the staff and students. The steps below are based on my experience in accomplishing my vision for the department: to strive for excellence, to go for the gold.

1. Organize yourself. "Time is gold," according to a Malay proverb, so use it wisely. I had to not only manage the department but also teach a group of MA students; supervise a group of BA, MA, and PhD students; mentor BA and MA students; serve on committees; and attend to other responsibilities and commitments. The list was endless. Luckily, however, I had an efficient assistant who called me every morning to remind me about things I had to do—attend meetings, meet with people, and more. She would jot down the important dates on the white board inside my office and on the one in hers. I then marked the dates in my personal diary, on my computer, and on the wall planner and refrigerator door at home. Even so, I missed one or two important meetings and appointments. After a few months I managed to organize myself and, eventually, began to smile a bit more as I got used to all these schedules. This type of organization seems to work well for me, but each person has a different style of organization; something that works well for one might not work as well for another.

2. Understand the staff members. My department offers many language courses (e.g., Japanese, Spanish, Korean, Dutch, Vietnamese, Burmese, Thai, German, Chinese, French, and Arabic), so the staff members come from all over the world. The first thing I did when I became the head was to call an informal meeting to get to know them. I was at first apprehensive about trying to understand people from different cultural backgrounds and experiences. Most of the staff were older and had more teaching experience than I. Needless to say, I felt a bit inferior. I overcame this by offering them my friendship. My door was open, and I was ready to listen to their problems, whether academic, student-related, or personal. They were also free to call me at the office, at home, or on my cell phone.

3. Adopt a bottom-up management style. This style of generating change from the bottom to the top was effective in our department. We organized meetings or brainstorming sessions to share ideas for course materials, which resulted in innovative teaching materials, a monitoring system for exams, ways to motivate the students, and suggestions for becoming more effective teachers. I appointed coordinators who served as line managers to directly supervise how things were going. Other staff members were expected to cooperate with the coordinators to ensure that things would run smoothly.

4. Understand the students. Students are the department's clients, so it is important to cater to their needs and requests. Try to understand their learning preferences by getting the teachers to administer learning style surveys. This surveying, which can take place any time during the course, gives administrators an indication of students' current attitudes and needs. Using the information from the surveys, you can identify useful materials and exercises as well as ineffective and outdated activities. The surveys also indicate the students' levels of interest and whether they are bored with certain materials and pedagogy.

5. Share the rewards of the department's success with the staff members. I found that a good way of doing this was to reinforce positive actions with verbal and written rewards and to eliminate negative efforts with direct constructive criticism.

This approach tends to produce a more comfortable environment for both head and staff members. Lunch outings, memos, and thank-you cards can be satisfying ways to recognize individuals who have made strong efforts to improve the department. I believe that this kind of work environment makes employees feel safe to make mistakes, as they will not be punished for doing so.

6. Encourage the spirit of working together. In managing an academic department, I needed all the help I could get from staff members. I formed a committee to monitor the quality of exam papers, vet the exam questions, and make sure there were no errors in the papers; another to monitor the courses and course materials; and another to revise certain courses because they were no longer suitable. Another committee arranged logistics, such as venues, presentation schedules, and refreshments, for seminars and workshops at which experts from other universities gave talks and exchanged ideas on ways to teach a foreign language. Additionally, we planned events such as Foreign Language Day, Japanese Day, and French Day. These events were a means to attract students to enroll in the department's courses, which are elective, and to motivate those who were already enrolled.

7. Adopt a hands-on management style. As the head, do not shy away from the students and staff. I often walked in the hallways to get firsthand information from the staff and students. I also visited classrooms to observe the teaching (after getting permission from the teachers), and to see whether the students were motivated to learn and the classrooms were comfortable (e.g., whether the air conditioning system was working properly and the furniture was in good condition).

8. Exchange ideas with other administrators. Each of the four departments in my faculty has a department head, a dean, and two deputy deans. We usually meet once a week—often over coffee—to discuss administrative matters and learn from one another.

9. Encourage interdepartmental cooperation. I encouraged my staff members to work with the staff from other departments.

Because we sometimes needed help monitoring exam papers but did not have the expertise in testing among our department staff, we invited experts from other departments to attend the committee meetings. I also encouraged staff members to collaborate with staff from other departments or faculties on research. For example, when an instructor from my department wanted to do a research project on computer-assisted language learning, I encouraged the instructor to collaborate with a computer expert from another department. Encouraging interdepartmental cooperation often motivates people to take on new projects and assignments and complete them on time.

10. Encourage the professional development of the staff members. The academic staff members of my department are either language instructors (first degree holders) or lecturers (with an MA or PhD). I called the language instructors to my office one by one to discuss their futures, encouraging them to continue their studies at the postgraduate level so that they could be appointed as lecturers. I urged lecturers without PhDs to work on a PhD full or part time. The teaching staff also took courses related to foreign language teaching and attended workshops, conferences (where they were encouraged to present papers based on their research or classroom experiences), and seminars locally or abroad. The university supports the professional development of the academic staff members; sponsorship is guaranteed if they wish to attend seminars or conferences as long as they present papers.

Conclusion

Managing an academic department is a demanding and challenging job, especially for someone who, like me, has no management background. However, looking back on my years as an administrator, I feel especially grateful for the ways the experience has changed my life. The demands and challenges as an administrator have made me a stronger and wiser person than the ESL instructor who once walked into the dean's office. I am more responsible toward my superiors, colleagues, and students. When I am given a job to do, I try my best to deliver it and, of course, to deliver it on time. I now know how it feels to wait for people to do things for you and how upset you can get if deadlines are not met. I hope that the principles that I have learned to value will help other administrators appreciate the importance of organizational management in improving the effectiveness of their departments.

Resources

Lindholm, J. (1999). *Preparing department chairs for their leadership roles* (ERIC Digest). Retrieved January 15, 2002, from http://www.ed.gov/databases/ERIC_Digests/ed433870.html (ERIC Document Reproduction Service No. ED433870)

Seagren, A. T., et al. (1993). *The department chair: New roles, responsibilities and challenges* (ERIC Digest). Retrieved January 15, 2002, from http://www.ed.gov/databases/ERIC_Digests/ed363165.html (ERIC Document Reproduction Service No. ED363165)

Contributor

Siti Hamin Stapa (sitihami@pkrisc.cc.ukm.my) is the former head of the Foreign Language Studies Department, Faculty of Language Studies, at the National University of Malaysia. Her main interests are the teaching of writing to ESL students, computer-mediated communication, and ESL methodology.

9 A Far Cry From the Classroom: Becoming an Administrator

Rosslyn Smith

Narrative

When I first walked into a Spanish classroom more than 30 years ago, I never imagined that I would eventually find myself being a full-time university administrator. As a teaching assistant at the University of New Mexico in the early 1970s, I discovered a love for teaching and a real joy in working with students. When I obtained my first full-time faculty position at West Virginia University, however, I found that, although teaching was the most important part of my job, I also acquired program development and administrative responsibilities, such as setting up and administering an English language testing program for international students and collaborating in the development of an intensive English program (IEP).

In 1979, after 5 years at West Virginia University, I moved to Texas Tech University and into a half-time teaching, half-time administrative position as director of ESL programs. What that meant for me was establishing and directing the international teaching assistant (ITA) program and the IEP; administering the English language testing program for international students; and teaching Spanish, linguistics, and academic ESL courses. In 1995, I became the founding director of a faculty and instructional development center at Texas Tech, a one-third teaching, two-thirds administrative position. More recently, in 2000, I moved into a full-time administrative position as interim and then vice provost for outreach and extended studies, a far cry from the Spanish classroom I had entered over 30 years ago.

As is true for many ESL and non-ESL faculty colleagues that I know, nothing in my doctoral work had prepared me for these administrative roles—my preparation was on-the-job training, experience, reading, learning from my many mistakes, and having professional development opportunities along the way.

Description

For years I have heard faculty members mutter about "the administration" and at times joined in, setting up what I now believe to be a mostly false adversarial relationship between faculty and administrators. As a faculty member, I was responsible for teaching, advising, research, and service. As an administrator, I am responsible for creating an environment in which people can do their jobs with a minimum of interference and a maximum amount of support. To that end, I am accountable for seeing that operating policies and procedures are known and followed; that resources are responsibly managed and distributed according to program need; that supervisors who report to me receive adequate training to improve their skills; that the activities, goals, and achievements of my area are accurately reported; and that my area contributes to the success of the institutional strategic goals and initiatives. I see the roles of faculty members and administrators as complementary, not adversarial.

What does it take to move from a predominantly faculty role into a predominantly administrative role? This question has many equally valid answers. The steps I describe below reflect my experiences and the lessons I learned as I took on new roles.

Moving Into Administration

The following ideas are for those who are not currently involved in administration but would like to move in that direction.

1. Be known for your integrity. Tell the truth. If you make a mistake, admit it. Give credit where credit is due, and do not blame others for your own errors or oversights. No one expects you to be perfect, but everyone needs to be able to trust what you say.

2. Carefully analyze your strengths and weaknesses before moving into an administrative role. Consider whether you like doing paperwork, writing reports, attending meetings, and making policy decisions. Does confrontation make you uncomfortable? Do you have good ideas that you would like to implement? Is teaching your first priority?

3. Analyze your institutional and departmental culture. Think about the kind of administration you would like to do and how it is perceived on your campus. Do you come from a unit that has been historically marginalized? Do you meet institutional criteria for being an administrator? Who are the stakeholders in the administrative area you would like to work in, and how would they react if you became an administrator in that area? How are administrators perceived in general in your institutional context?

4. Start with something manageable. Consider seeking opportunities to perform administrative tasks within your existing position. Perhaps you can take on some extra advising responsibilities or records management. You might look for appropriate college- or university-level committees to serve on. Run for the faculty senate, and serve on senate committees. Get to know people outside your unit, and develop an understanding of their needs and priorities.

5. Do your homework. If you want to make an impression on those who are in a position to give you more administrative tasks, be prepared in your discussions. For example, before you

propose a new program, find out what others are doing, make a plan on the basis of your institutional situation, build consensus among your stakeholders, and write your plan so that someone who is not in your field can understand it. Be patient and polite, but be persistent.

6. Know the rules and follow them. Familiarize yourself with the institutional operating policies. Find out which policies affect your unit and how the policies can facilitate your work. Often, the most successful administrators are those who understand how the system works and know how to use the rules in support of their goals and objectives.

7. Take advantage of professional development opportunities. If your institution has a training or professional development office, contact that office to see how you might benefit from short courses or workshops it provides. Professional associations such as TESOL and NAFSA: Association of International Educators offer a multitude of professional development opportunities. Apply for travel funds to attend workshops; go to as many local, state, regional, and national conferences as you can; talk to colleagues from other institutions; learn what the national context is for whatever administrative task you have in mind. Affiliate with others in administrative positions, such as members of TESOL's Program Administration or International Teaching Assistants interest sections or NAFSA's Administrators and Teachers in English as a Second Language section. One of the first major professional development opportunities I was able to take advantage of was a 3-day NAFSA postconference workshop on administrative skills development in 1980. Since then, these organizations have afforded me the opportunity to learn additional administrative, consulting, leadership, and organizational development skills.

Consider joining related nondisciplinary professional associations. In my role with the Teaching, Learning, and Technology Center, I have found that the Professional and Organizational Development Network in Higher Education (POD) has given me new insights and introduced me to colleagues in faculty and instructional development. The American Association for Higher Education (AAHE) provides numerous workshops and conferences related to issues in higher education. Do some research to learn what the opportunities are, and then get involved. Also take advantage of the professional publications sponsored by organizations such as TESOL, NAFSA, AAHE, and POD.

8. Volunteer. Make yourself an integral part of your institution and unit. If you see that someone needs help with a task, offer to help. If you see something that needs to be done, offer to do it. People notice and appreciate a genuine can-do, helpful attitude.

Being an Administrator

If you assume administrative responsibilities, you might consider the following ideas.

1. Never blindside your boss. You will encounter a host of potentially sticky or delicate situations that may have implications for your supervisors. Get in the habit of giving people a heads-up when something might be coming their way. If you get a call from an irate parent or student who wants to talk to your supervisor, let your boss know what is coming and provide some background by telephone or e-mail. In this area especially, your boss must have confidence in your integrity and willingness to present difficult situations fairly.

2. Focus on issues, not personalities. Whether you administer a small unit or one with several hundred employees, you will spend more time than you ever dreamed possible handling personnel issues, conflicts, and competing interests. When a conflict arises, and it will, try to focus on the issues that underlie the situation. Listen carefully to what people tell you, and avoid leaping to conclusions without having all the information you need. Remember that you do not have to solve everything at once.

3. Make communication a priority. Your success as an administrator will be greatly affected by how well you communicate your vision and plans. Poor or infrequent

communication often leads to misunderstandings, frustration, and resentment, all of which will make your job much more difficult.

4. Mind your own administrative business. Few things make others as angry as having people who might not know all the facts jump into the middle of something that does not concern them. To the extent possible, stay out of other units' internal disputes.

5. Pick your fights. Do not turn every disagreement into a bitter dispute. Take a stand if you need to, but, in general, try not to alienate people you will need to work with later to accomplish your goals. Sometimes you can agree to disagree without compromising your principles or your program.

6. Take care of yourself. Administration is not glamorous. Many of the administrators I know regularly spend far more than 40 hours a week at the office and attend 10–25 or more meetings a week. If you want to maintain your mental and physical health, you will need to find a way to achieve some balance in your life.

7. Maintain a healthy perspective on who you are and what you do. Try not to take yourself too seriously, such as thinking that it is all about you when it is not or that you are indispensable when you are not. As administrators, our goal should be to create an environment in which we are not indispensable; that fosters creativity, fairness, and excellence; and in which people can function effectively whether we are there or not.

Conclusion

For some, the worst part of administration is not spending time with students in and out of the classroom; for others, it is feeling distant from more traditional academic roles and not having adequate time to spend on research. Administrators must also expect criticism, some of which can be biting and painful. There are often personnel issues to deal with as well as one's own occasional feelings of insecurity and inadequacy. On the positive side, being an administrator can be very rewarding. I have found it exciting to start new programs and watch them develop, or to confront difficult situations and see them improve. I have learned new skills and acquired new knowledge, interacted with and learned from colleagues at institutions all over the country and abroad, and grown personally and professionally. If you decide to ease into a new role as an administrator, you may have the opportunity to make a real difference in something you care about in ways that you might not otherwise have had available.

Resources

American Association for Higher Education (AAHE). http:// www.aahe.org

> AAHE's members are primarily faculty, administrators, and students who are concerned about challenging issues in higher education. Several of AAHE's in-depth initiatives focus on assessment, faculty roles, quality, teaching, and service learning. AAHE's Web site highlights these initiatives and provides information on its publications and other resources.

NAFSA: Association of International Educators. http://www.nafsa.org

> NAFSA brings together professionals in all areas of international education. One of NAFSA's five professional sections is Administrators and Teachers in English as a Second Language (ATESL). Browse NAFSA's Web site for information about its professional sections and publications.

Professional and Organizational Development Network in Higher Education (POD). http://www.podnetwork.org

> POD is an active organization consisting primarily of professionals in faculty, instructional, and organizational development. The Web site provides information about POD's mission and activities and links to valuable resources and publications.

TESOL. http://www.tesol.org

> Several of TESOL's interest sections would appeal to administrators, such as ESL in Higher Education, Program Administration, and International Teaching Assistants. Browse the Web site for information on the focus and activities of the interest sections as well as on TESOL publications.

Contributor

Rosslyn Smith (rosslyn.smith@ttu.edu) is vice provost for outreach and extended studies, director of the Teaching, Learning, and Technology Center, and a faculty member at Texas Tech University in Lubbock, Texas, in the United States. She is the former director of the international teaching assistant and intensive English programs, and her current responsibilities include the administration of instructional development programs for faculty and teaching assistants. She is coauthor of *Crossing Pedagogical Oceans: International Teaching Assistants in U.S. Undergraduate Education* (1992; ERIC Document Reproduction Service No. ED358812) and has served as a commissioner for the Commission on English Language Program Accreditation.

10 Taking the Bull by the Horns: Designing a Teacher-Initiated Professional Development Program

Elana Spector-Cohen, Carol Wexler, and Sara Kol

Narrative

It was June 1999. As teachers streamed into the conference room, we nervously wondered if the miniconference, the culminating activity of the first project in our program, would be all that we hoped for. During the first 2 years of the in-service program, the 50 English teachers in the department had collaborated in small working committees to explore problematic issues relevant to our English for academic purposes (EAP) program. After more than 2 years of struggling with these issues, each committee was about to present its findings at a full-day miniconference. The committee work culminating in the conference was the first project in a series aimed at promoting ongoing professionalism among the teachers in our department. Other projects were to follow. Our vision of a viable, sustainable, in-service program was becoming a reality.

The conference began. Would it be a success? Would the teachers take their tasks seriously? Would their presentations be well received by their colleagues? We scanned the sea of faces, looking for signs of enthusiasm rather than resistance. One after the other, staff members, some of whom had never presented in any academic forum, stood up and addressed the pedagogical issues pertinent to our context: What constitutes a good reading comprehension test? How much vocabulary should we teach explicitly at the advanced levels? Should we incorporate writing and speaking in our courses? What are the special language needs of new immigrants? What criteria should be applied to teacher observation? As each teacher stood up and walked to the podium, we held our breaths. Each time, our fears were quickly allayed as the speaker began to talk. The presentations were professional, highly informative, and creative. We looked around the room, and our colleagues' faces beamed with pride and satisfaction. We felt a great sense of accomplishment at our own part in creating this crowning moment. And this was only the beginning; additional projects to enhance professionalism were waiting in the wings.

Description

It all began in the summer of 1997, when the three of us informally discussed the problems we were encountering as university language instructors and course coordinators. We assumed that other teachers in the department might be experiencing similar frustrations. Perhaps, together, we could tackle the professional issues within the context of an in-service program. However, previous attempts at in-service development had been sporadic and had lacked a comprehensive vision. Hence, the key issue was how to involve all 50 staff members in their own professional development, not only by enhancing their functioning in the classroom, but also by attending conferences, reading the professional literature, and conducting research. However, who were we to expect to make the sweeping changes necessary to involve everyone in such an ambitious endeavor? Although we were experienced teachers, we had limited background in teacher education and had not been formally appointed to undertake such a task. Still, we decided to take the bull by the horns and organize a professional development program. We wrote a proposal, which was accepted by the head of the department. Then we applied for a university grant and got it. The wheels were set in motion.

The first step in establishing an ongoing professional development program was to create a pedagogical committee to oversee the program. The committee was composed of eight teachers, with rotating memberships. This setup assured maximum teacher involvement and participation at all levels of our in-service program. Once established, the pedagogical committee determined the overall goals of the staff development program, namely, to enhance professionalism, bridge the gap between theory and practice, and encourage participation in professional academic discourse.

The initial in-service project that culminated in the miniconference involved the creation of seven working committees to explore issues relevant to our context. The committees were asked to make recommendations and suggestions for pedagogical changes, so almost the entire staff was involved in the decision-making process. The committees explored the topics of (a) testing, (b) materials and syllabus evaluation, (c) criteria for teacher evaluation, (d) oral-aural skills, (e) writing, (f) advanced English for specific purposes courses, and (g) classroom management. The committees' findings were written up in a report, presented to the staff at the miniconference, and collected in a booklet that was distributed to staff members for future reference. The pedagogical committee was then responsible for implementing the working committees' recommendations. This process completed our first in-service project but did not mark the end of our program.

If we wanted to sustain professionalism, we needed to ensure that the in-service program would be ongoing. Therefore, additional projects followed. The next one involved small reading groups, in which members read, discussed, and reported on current literature in the field, and subsequently chose to read in depth on a specific topic. At this writing, we are embarking on a new project that involves the creation of a virtual teachers' room, in which reading group members will present the findings of their research and interact with other members of the department. In addition, teachers will be able to communicate, discuss pedagogical issues, and share materials and ideas online.

Outcomes of our overall professional development program have been a growing sense of professional competence, increased collaboration and collegiality, and a shared body of knowledge, all of which have fostered a greater willingness to experiment with new ideas in the classroom. Most significantly, the in-service program has led to an overall improvement in staff professionalism; more staff members are presenting at national and international conferences and writing for publication.

Steps

Based on our experience with and reflections on the evolution of our ongoing professional development program, we recommend the following steps for designing a similar program.

1. Take the initiative; be proactive. If you feel that your context could benefit from an enhanced in-service program, take the bull by the horns and make a proposal. Who knows the needs of your institution better than you do? If a gap really exists and your proposal fills it, then your plan has a good chance of being accepted.

2. Seek formal institutional recognition for your program. The institutional structure must be conducive to professional development. If need be, create or recommend the formation of an official body that will be responsible for planning and coordinating activities. This body will help keep your program on track. Teachers should serve on this body on a rotating basis to allow for collaborative leadership.

3. Require all staff members to participate. Our experience as teachers, learners, and human beings has taught us that sometimes people need to be forced to realize their potential. Required participation in the program relays the message that professional development is a top priority in the department or institution. Expect some resistance, particularly from more experienced staff members. However, if you can capitalize on their skills and experience, for example, as group leaders or mentors, you may be able to gain their cooperation.

4. Rely on familiarity with your setting. You do not always need to depend on outside experts, who are not necessarily familiar with your specific needs. A program generated from within your

institution will be not only relevant but most likely self-sustaining and, thus, ongoing.

5. Keep your in-service program on site. An on-site program will be logistically simpler and more cost-effective. In addition, try to set aside a weekly time slot when no teaching takes place for professional development.

6. Elicit staff suggestions and reactions. Such input ensures teacher participation at every stage of the program. You can get this information through questionnaires, informal discussions with teachers, and requests for ideas and materials.

7. Use your expertise as a teacher. Your program can be planned and directed by teachers. In a higher education setting, leading a professional development program involves principles and skills of effective learning and teaching similar to those applied in the classroom. Moreover, utilizing effective methodology in in-service activities could lead to a positive backwash effect on classroom teaching.

8. Devise a clearly defined goal at each stage of the project, and make the goal clear to all participants. For example, one of our goals was to encourage all staff members to keep abreast of current professional literature.

9. Create a series of relevant, intellectually stimulating subtasks that will facilitate the attainment of the goal. For example, we compiled a reading list consisting of teacher-recommended articles. We then devised a number of tasks in which groups of teachers read and reacted to the articles and presented their conclusions and insights to the entire staff.

10. Devise a final product that serves as the culminating activity for each project. Assigning a final product conveys the seriousness of the task.

11. Establish deadlines for each stage of the process. You may find that your deadlines need to be extended, but having a deadline will sustain momentum.

12. Organize the participants into small groups. We found that groups of about five to eight members worked best. In such a

framework, participants are more likely to feel involved and have the opportunity to express themselves. This is particularly pertinent for staff members who do not readily speak in larger forums. Moreover, in small groups, individual members take greater responsibility for completing tasks, as responsibility is less diffused. The group process breaks down the barriers among people and encourages new working relationships.

13. Reassemble all the groups into one large forum. At our final meeting, each group presented its final product to the entire staff. Such a gathering gives teachers an opportunity to share what they have learned and creates a common knowledge base among the staff members. Second, knowing that their small group is expected to give an oral presentation sustains group momentum and increases accountability among members. Third, presenting to colleagues can validate a teacher's sense of professional growth. The final forum simulates an authentic academic gathering and provides a springboard for presenting at national and international conferences as well as writing for academic publications. Finally, the forum encourages collegiality and bonding, pride in the workplace, and a sense of unity.

Conclusion

In the beginning, we had no idea where this professional development program would take us. Something had to be done to move the department forward in a collaborative effort. Consensus and cooperation were important in order to minimize potential resistance, as we were embarking on a program that would require the participation of all staff members. In reality, about 10% of the staff members have not actively participated, and this disparity remains an unresolved issue. Today we are still grappling with a dynamic program that is constantly evolving, but now we have the self-confidence to provide the professional development that enriches the department and keeps us reflecting. The overall program is now firmly established, and we, as founders of and participants in the program, expect to sustain professionalism, together with our colleagues.

Although the main goal of our program is to promote professional development among the staff, we ourselves have experienced a similar growth and sense of personal satisfaction. Specifically, we have researched, presented, and written on the topic of in-service development; we have learned about group dynamics and leadership, and how to identify and respond effectively to the needs of our department. Indeed, we have experienced an increased sense of empowerment and a growing awareness that we can affect our environment.

Resources

Bailey, K., Curtis, A., & Nunan, D. (1998). Undeniable insights: The collaborative use of three professional development practices. *TESOL Quarterly, 32,* 546–555.

Hare, A. P. (1982). *Creativity in small groups.* Beverly Hills, CA: Sage.

Kirschner, M., Spector-Cohen, E., & Wexler, C. (1996). A teacher education workshop on the construction of EFL tests and materials. *TESOL Quarterly, 30,* 85–111.

Smylie, M. A. (1995). Teacher learning in the workplace. In T. R. Guskey & M. Huberman (Eds.), *Professional development in education: New paradigms and practices* (pp. 92–131). New York: Teachers College Press.

Contributors

Elana Spector-Cohen (espector@internet-zahav.net) coordinates and teaches English for academic purposes courses in the Division of Foreign Languages at Tel Aviv University, in Israel, and is the senior coordinator of the Preacademic Program. She has collaborated with colleagues on presentations and publications in the fields of testing, professional development, curriculum design, and the use of e-mail in cross-cultural communication.

Carol Wexler (wexlercarol@hotmail.com) is a teacher and course coordinator of advanced-level English for academic purposes courses at Tel Aviv University, in Israel. She teaches English for specific purposes reading courses to students of architecture, art history, East

Asian studies, and geography. She has collaborated with colleagues on presentations and publications in the fields of testing, professional development, and curriculum design.

Sara Kol (sarakol@bezeqint.net) coordinates and teaches advanced-level English for academic purposes courses in the Division of Foreign Languages at Tel Aviv University, in Israel, and is a member of the academic staff of the university language learning center. She heads the team that is developing Web sites for the English language courses. Her research interests include screen reading and academic literacies as well as the use of Web-based components to enhance language learning.

11

Training Teachers to Be Teacher Trainers: It's More Complicated Than You'd Think

Briony Beaven

Narrative

I believe that teachers have much to share with and learn from other teachers, so I recently designed a program in which teachers in our adult education institute ran workshops to share their expertise with colleagues. Workshops could focus on a type of class, a set of materials, a language area, or a classroom dynamics issue. To get the program started, I invited specific teachers to lead workshops. For example, one teacher, who had written a master's thesis on using visual aids in the EFL classroom, brought her materials and described how she used them in class. The participants seemed happy with their new resources, but I had some concerns about the organization and presentation of the workshop materials. Then, another teacher in our program called me to say she had taught many classes of a particular type and was eager to present a workshop. She seemed extremely confident about what she would do in the workshop. We discussed some of the content but did not cover the aims or processes.

As the workshop got underway, the teacher still looked confident, but I was worried that she had not given any prior thought to an appropriate arrangement of the furniture in the room. As the 3 hours slowly passed, I realized that the workshop was becoming a disaster. The attendees were overwhelmed by hundreds of photocopies and were given little time to discuss what to do with the materials, the reasons for using them, or the philosophy of learning implicit in them. The teachers were polite and tried to participate, but an atmosphere of discontent and unease prevailed. One teacher commented as we sat uneasily together during a partner activity with poor instructions, "I'm sure you didn't mean the workshop to be like this!" No, I certainly had not. After that unfortunate afternoon, I wondered if my idea of peer teacher education was no more than lip service to a currently popular idea. It seemed that I had exposed an unsuspecting teacher to embarrassment and failure and had wasted the time of her colleagues, who were freelance and were not being paid for attending the workshop. The other first few workshops were more successful than this one, but the teachers who led them said afterward that they felt they could have done a better job. They needed to know more about working as teacher educators.

Description

The literature on teacher education suggests that people often enter the field by chance. As Wallace (1991) states, "many of us who started our careers as language teachers find ourselves in the position of being trainers of language teachers," and, as a result, "may see ourselves as operating outside our area of expertise" (p. 4). Novice teacher educators commonly have to learn how to instruct others on their own, although they would like guidance. One teacher who became a teacher educator said, "I have had no specific training for this job, ... I feel I need specific training, especially in facilitating skills" (Durham, 2001, p. 6). However, teachers frequently do become teacher educators. My own experience provides a not uncommon example. I attended a short training course on preservice teacher education, took my first steps as an in-service educator through an informal apprenticeship with a senior colleague, and added to my theoretical knowledge about teacher education through the language teacher education module in my doctoral program.

As a next step, I wanted to find a way to help other classroom teachers learn to be teacher educators so that they could share their knowledge and experience. How could teachers who wanted to run workshops gain at least some insight into strategies for effective teacher education in a short time and at a low cost? What they really needed was a course on some aspects of teacher education. However, as freelancers, they needed to spend most of their time on paid work. Because I strongly believe in the teacher-as-educator model as a means to professional development in our context, I developed a brief workshop that provided an introduction to teacher education.

Steps

If you work in a context similar to mine and are interested in helping teachers become teacher educators, you may find the following steps applicable.

1. Work within the system to help teachers become the teacher educators the school or program needs. For example, my workshop was designed with the recognition that our school and teachers did not have the time or money for a large-scale education program. (For a description of a larger-scale program, see chapter 10 in this volume.) Thus, I decided to build the program around brief in-service sessions.

2. Ground the workshop firmly in what is known about teacher learning, and discuss your decisions with the participants. As you prepare your workshop, read as much as you can in the literature on teacher education, with a special emphasis on effective ways to prepare classroom teachers to become teacher educators (see the Resources section). I also discussed with the workshop participants the thinking process that had gone into planning the workshop and presented it to them as a rationale for the workshop content. Making your thinking explicit may allow others to use it as a model in designing their own workshops. For example, I rejected a recipe-style approach for my first session, even though it was tempting, given the limited

time. The second session, however, involved some necessary nuts and bolts. I believed the participants would benefit more by doing in-depth thinking before seeing the recipes.

3. Decide on the key issues that prospective teacher educators need to be aware of. My reading, assumptions, experiences, and beliefs resulted in a workshop that I describe below as an example of one kind of introduction to teacher education. I included the following topics:

   - reflection on the participants' experiences of what they consider to be good teacher education

   - clarification of the participants' definitions of learning, teaching, and teacher education

   - discussion of the relevance of teachers' beliefs to their learning

   - comparison of the knowledge and skills needed by a teacher educator with those needed by a classroom language teacher

   - consideration of relationships between content and presentation processes for the workshops that the participants would design for fellow teachers

   - presentation of a reflective cycle model for the teacher educators' professional development

4. Make the aims of the session explicit to the participants. The teachers had enrolled, we discovered, expecting a session devoted entirely to practical matters in teacher education workshops, such as selection of topics, timing of presentations, and interaction patterns. I realized that I needed to help potential workshop participants have a clearer understanding of the purposes and methods of this teacher education workshop at the outset.

5. Ask the participants who attend your first workshop to give you feedback, and use it to prepare your next workshop. The participants at my first workshop said they had found it rewarding to think about key issues, and they thought we had learned a great deal from one another. We agreed that listening to each other had helped us develop and extend our own

thinking. Furthermore, the group expressed a feeling of ease and openness. Nevertheless, the teachers decided they would need to do more work before running their own sessions and that they would like to stay together for a continuation of the course. If you want to provide ongoing opportunities for teachers to learn to share their knowledge and skills with peers, then build into the first workshop an opportunity for the participants to decide on additional steps. It may even be possible to fix a date for the next workshop while the participants are with you and in the first flush of enthusiasm.

6. Have a plan for dealing with access to workshops if prior preparation and attendance are important to its design. The participants in the first workshop designed the second one, building on the relationships and knowledge developed in that initial session. However, our institution works on an open-access basis and requires that we publish events for teachers in a printed program. Thus, I had to decide what to do if newcomers wanted to join the second workshop. We decided to admit newcomers if they did some initial homework. To this end, I prepared and mailed to newcomers versions of our workshop tasks adapted for individual study and an introduction to the group. The program description for the second workshop stated clearly that newcomers needed to register and prepare the precourse tasks.

   Nevertheless, I was faced with an unregistered attendee, who had been encouraged to come by one of the newly registered attendees. I decided that, in spite of our usual open-arms policy, the basis for this second workshop was the jointly constructed knowledge and the social relationships created in the first. I explained to the would-be attendee that she could not stay and why. Although your decision may be different, you will need to establish a policy regarding nonregistered attendees if the success of your workshop depends on preparation carried out in advance of the workshop by registered participants.

7. Plan and run subsequent sessions according to the previous workshops, the expressed needs of the participants, and your

and the participants' views of issues that should be explored. Our second workshop included discussion of additional topics important for teachers who want to become teacher educators. In this follow-up session, the group also moved from theoretical matters to more practical issues in workshop design, including

- different values and goals in teacher education
- the effects of those values on planning a workshop for teachers
- facilitation styles and process options
- topic choice
- organizational matters, such as publicity, room arrangements, refreshments, types of participants, visual and aural aids, session introduction, handouts, feedback, and content
- ways of creating a tactful, nonauthoritarian, in-service classroom through the choice of language, in particular the use of modal adverbs, modal auxiliaries, and references to authorities other than oneself
- concrete tips, workable procedures, and caveats for the successful training of experienced classroom teachers

Thus, we delved into issues of theory and belief but also explored their implications for the organization and content of teacher education workshops, along with other practical matters.

Conclusion

Working in a context in which one is pleased if teachers sacrifice even one half-day for professional development, I had expected to present a single workshop session. Although one participant ran a teachers' workshop soon after our train-the-trainer sessions, others still did not think that they were ready to offer workshops for fellow teachers. As one said, "It's more complicated than you'd think, isn't it?" Her comment suggests that an overview of the knowledge and skills required by teacher educators can initially undermine teachers' confidence in their ability to lead workshops. Better this initial doubt,

I would suggest, followed by a renewal of confidence based on tangible skills, than misplaced confidence, which can lead to bad workshop experiences, such as the one described at the beginning of this chapter. As a result of the session, I expected some of the participants eventually to lead teacher workshops, and felt they had sufficient confidence, skills, and knowledge to do this well. Others, I thought, might never take that step, but through a better understanding of their educators' role and concerns, they might be able to learn more from workshops they attend as participants.

Our course began, and yours may begin, as an emergency train-the-trainer program, designed to prevent disasters. However, once I became aware of the need for this course, it seemed a good opportunity for me as well as the participating teachers to develop professionally. Teaching anything, of course, means knowing it in quite a different way from attempting to understand it for oneself. My first workshop and its follow-up session provided a chance for me to embed my recent theoretical learning in practice. I was afraid of putting on a borrowed coat that might be much too big for me, but was lucky in beginning with an understanding group of teachers with whom I could share the uncertainties of my new role and discuss my decision-making processes. The participants and I put on borrowed coats together, all of us starting a new job informally, I as a trainer of trainers and the teachers as trainers of other teachers, choosing to do so because of our wish to move beyond routine.

Resources

You may devise some of the tasks for your prospective teacher educators, but you may also use published materials; I used the following sources for some of the tasks in my train-the-trainer course.

Durham, J. (2001). Becoming a teacher educator. *The Teacher Trainer,* *15*(2), 4–7.

Gough, B., & James, D. (1990). *Planning professional training days.* Milton Keynes, England: Open University Press.

> Most teachers moving into teacher education are concerned with good organization as well as appropriate content and processes. This book, particularly pp. 76–85, provides sensible guidance on practical aspects of short teacher courses.

James, P. (2001). *Teachers in action*. Cambridge: Cambridge University Press.

Teacher educators need to be aware of different views of the purposes of teacher education. They need to know what purposes they think their own classrooms are serving. James's metaphor task (pp. 35–38) for uncovering teachers' views of their classrooms can easily be adapted to uncover teacher educators' views of the training classroom.

Lubelska, D., & Robbins, L. (1999, November). Moving from teaching to training. *The IATEFL Teacher Trainers' SIG Newsletter, 3*, 7–9.

Malderez, A., & Bodoczky, C. (1999). *Mentor courses*. Cambridge: Cambridge University Press.

Teacher education frequently aims to change teacher behavior. A joint reconstruction of the iceberg diagram in this source (p. 15) helps future teacher educators realize how teacher behavior is influenced by values, beliefs, and feelings.

Roberts, J. (1998). *Language teacher education*. London: Arnold.

Wallace, M. J. (1991). *Training foreign language teachers: A reflective approach*. Cambridge: Cambridge University Press.

Contributor

Briony Beaven (brionybeaven@compuserve.com) is the director of studies in the English Department of the Münchner Volkshochschule, in Munich, Germany, where she teaches adult learners of English, organizes and serves as trainer in the teacher education program, observes lessons, and counsels teachers. She also writes course books and enjoys contributing to professional journals. She is currently studying for an EdD TEFL at the University of Exeter.

12 Sabbatical Projects Can Make a Difference: A Tale of Curriculum Revision

Sharon Seymour

Narrative

When I told my colleagues and my husband that I wanted to spend time on campus for my sabbatical project, they all said, "You're crazy!" "You should be doing something that keeps you away from this place," my colleagues said. "You should be doing a travel sabbatical so we can take a trip somewhere," my husband said.

I had spent a semester in Europe and a semester studying at another college in the United States for an earlier sabbatical, so I felt I had already used those options. Moreover, I had become interested in the role of reading in academic programs after reading an article in *TESOL Quarterly* (Shih, 1992). I therefore put together a sabbatical proposal to study the reading challenges ESL students face in mainstream classes at the community college where I work. I thought I could gather information that would help my fellow ESL instructors, our program, and perhaps the college in general do a better job of preparing ESL students for college courses. However, I was pretty fuzzy at that point on how to effect any real change.

89

I took my sabbatical in spring 1996 and 1997 and presented the results of my study at a California TESOL conference, at a TESOL convention, and on staff development day at my college. Although my report recommended some changes, I had not fleshed out any specific plans for accomplishing them. One might think I would have been able to jump right into implementing changes when I took over as chair of my department in fall 1997. On the contrary, even though I had gotten a taste of administrative responsibilities serving as interim chair in fall 1994 and 1995, during my first few years as chair I spent a good deal of time learning and struggling to stay on top of the day-to-day challenges of managing one of the largest ESL departments in the world. Besides, I had heard that you should spend at least the first year of administration observing how things currently work before attempting any major changes. Frankly, the sabbatical receded to the back of my mind, although occasionally someone would ask to look at my report. Little did I know that a couple of years later I would be coordinating a wholesale curriculum revision for our program, partly inspired by my sabbatical project.

Description

For the sabbatical project, I observed 11 content courses at our community college, specifically focusing on the reading demands placed on the students. I chose 10 courses that satisfy general education graduation requirements and 1 vocational course, all of which have a high enrollment of ESL students. My research included questions such as these: What are ESL students reading in mainstream courses? How much are they reading? How much time do they spend on the reading? How important is the reading? What other skills are important? How are ESL students assessed on what they read? How are they doing in mainstream courses? What factors affect their academic success? I gathered information by observing classes, interviewing and surveying the instructors and ESL students in the classes, and reviewing course materials. Based on the information, I made the following recommendations: (a) Academic ESL courses should integrate reading and writing instruction because writing assignments in mainstream courses often require students to respond to readings in some way, (b) readings in academic ESL courses should be the type that students will encounter in the disciplines in which they will take classes, (c) academic skills development needs to be emphasized in all ESL courses at our college, (d) reading should be emphasized, (e) students should be taught to synthesize material from different sources (e.g., from reading and lectures), and (f) we should teach and assess all higher order thinking skills in a variety of ways.

The transition from sabbatical project to curriculum revision came gradually. At a colloquium on community college issues at the TESOL convention in 1998, I was inspired by a colleague's story of a major curriculum change her department had undertaken. I also attended sessions on integrating reading and writing in the curriculum. Back home, I read a sabbatical report by a fellow faculty member on ESL programs at other community colleges throughout the United States. I listened to a colleague who was committed to the integration of reading and writing and wanted to see a change. Faculty members who had read or heard about my sabbatical report agreed with many of my recommendations. I finally realized that our institution, too, could make changes and decided to plant the seeds for change among the faculty that spring. My department colleagues and I started gathering information in fall 1998 and voted in spring 1999 to move ahead. Our target for implementation was fall 2002, which would give us 2 years to lay the groundwork and a third year to get course outlines approved and plan the conversion to the new program.

Steps

The following are the steps we took to achieve curriculum reform.

1. Get commitment to the need for real change. Change does not come easily, and you may have to convince everyone that it is worthwhile. Find others who share your passion for change so that you are not the lone voice proposing this upheaval to the program. You may face some real resistance to change from your own faculty, from other departments, or from the college. In my institution, some faculty in the English department perceived that proposed changes to increase our upper-level course hours and strengthen the reading component of the courses would adversely affect enrollment in English

department reading classes. Their concerns died down after research showed that very few ESL students enroll in those classes.

2. Do your homework. Draw up your goals and objectives for the project, and define your desired outcomes. Survey the faculty and students on the strengths and weaknesses of the current curriculum and possible changes. Do research on the current success of your program. If possible, get release time for someone to gather this information. I organized a task force to draw up the goals and objectives, conduct a faculty survey and student focus groups, review the research and data collected, and develop proposals for change. Eventually, the task force's work was turned over to the department's curriculum committee. During the third year, I was finally able to give someone 20% release as program revision implementation facilitator.

3. Inform all affected parties of your plans and get them to buy in. First, get the faculty to agree to move ahead with a change. Figure out who needs to know and be convinced of the need for change, and use pertinent information gathered in the homework phase. We had departmental meetings, sent memos, and talked in the halls. Then we voted on the alternative proposals the task force developed. Once we had faculty buy-in, we informed the rest of the college of our intentions. First was the English department, provoking a not entirely unexpected negative response that was eventually handled with research that showed that our plan would not harm its enrollment. We were particularly concerned about the counseling department's reaction, so we made several presentations at its meetings and were relieved that department members seemed receptive to our changes. We informed the dean of curriculum, the vice chancellor of instruction, and the chancellor, prompting a visit by representatives of the chancellor's office to discuss the potential impact on college enrollment and funding. We made a preview presentation of our overall plans to the college curriculum committee. We talked with the library and learning resources dean, learning assistance department chair, and

others to discuss the need for additional lab space on campus. We also consulted with the college employee relations department and the union on workload and working conditions issues.

4. Make sure you have the facilities you need for your new curriculum. Our plans included adding a required lab hour to the reading, writing, and grammar course at the top two levels of the new curriculum. ESL had never had its own lab at our college; rather, ESL students used facilities in the college learning assistance center. With the anticipated increase in lab use, we had to intensify our quest for an ESL computer lab because campus facilities were already nearing capacity. Fortunately, thanks to a couple of supportive administrators who recognized our plight, the college identified funds to establish a lab in time for the fall 2002 semester.

5. Deal with faculty concerns over major pedagogical changes. You will likely be proposing changes that may radically affect how courses are structured and taught. In our case, the most contentious issue was the proposal to make our courses content-based. In my sabbatical report, I recommended that academic ESL programs use readings typical of those used in mainstream courses. Our curriculum committee decided to go with a content-based approach and designated specific content areas for course material at each level. For example, the proposed areas for the top level were current events, humanities, ecology and environment, physical sciences, behavioral sciences, business, and the economy. Instructors wondered if they would have to suddenly become experts in fields such as business and economics and how they would find a textbook that would work with this curriculum. This reaction prompted me to reread materials on content-based ESL and, with the curriculum committee, rethink the direction we wanted to take. Our compromise on this issue was that course outlines would state that readings should come from certain designated or other appropriate areas and that readings from one area should constitute no more than 50% of the course assignments (mostly to prevent instructors from using only

literature for reading material). Another major shift was integrating reading, writing, and grammar instruction in the upper-level courses. Although we had had a few sections of integrated courses at several levels for several years, the concept of integrating reading, writing, and grammar may mean a different way of doing things for some instructors. Even though we have voted to make these changes and published overall curricular frameworks, which most instructors have approved, we suspect some instructors are still in denial about the changes they will have to make.

6. Do staff development. Help faculty become comfortable with the changes they will need to make and give them some tools to help them change. Invite outside experts if you can, and get members of your staff to do workshops. Figure out how to provide staff development for everyone, if possible. We offered workshops on school days, but, of course, not everyone could attend. We were finally able to get funding in spring 2002 to hire substitutes for those who teach during regularly scheduled staff development workshops. Our program revision implementation facilitator conducted these workshops, which included minipresentations by instructors who had piloted a more content-infused, integrated reading, writing, and grammar curriculum. We hoped to ease the transition by showing faculty that they may have already been using approaches that the new curriculum called for.

7. Take care of details, some of which are not so minor. In the final semester before implementation, we tried to make sure we had not forgotten any of the details, such as deciding how students would be promoted from the existing program to the new program and how to adjust the placement system for new students, getting revised course information into the catalog, informing the college community and students of the changes, scheduling the new classes (e.g., making sure we had rooms available for the new time configurations), and creating a new book list. We also requested new articulation agreements with 4-year colleges and, because we are a public institution, got approval from the state chancellor's office for the new courses.

Conclusion

Did we redo our curriculum because of my sabbatical report? No. But it was one of the inspirations that led me to propose a change when I became chair. Do you have to be a department chair to instigate change? Ultimately, you will need the buy-in of the department chair and faculty, but the proposal for change could come from any committed faculty member. Have we been successful? We implemented the new curriculum in fall 2002, so, at the time of this writing, we do not yet have sufficient data to evaluate the results of the change. Nonetheless, we are well on our way. Did I have a grand plan from the beginning for how to mastermind major curriculum change? No. Rather, it has been an organic, evolving process involving many faculty members. I am happy that my sabbatical report did not end up on a shelf somewhere. Those of us fortunate enough to have sabbaticals realize that they give us a chance to step back from day-to-day teaching to learn and grow as professionals. My project inspired my interest in the role of reading in the curriculum. I consider it a bonus that my sabbatical has helped effect change at my college. Many of my recommendations for change are reflected in our new curriculum. I have gotten more use out of my sabbatical work than I had ever anticipated, and implementing curriculum change has been the ultimate in professional development experiences.

Resources

Brown, J. D. (1995). *The elements of language curriculum: A systematic approach to program development.* Boston: Heinle & Heinle.

This book offers helpful chapters on curriculum revision, including information on needs analysis, goals and objectives, testing, materials, and program evaluation.

Shih, M. (1992). Beyond comprehension exercises in the ESL academic reading class. *TESOL Quarterly, 26,* 289–318.

This article inspired my sabbatical project.

Snow, M. A., & Brinton, D. M. (Eds.). (1997). *The content-based classroom: Perspectives on integrating language and content.* Essex, England: Addison Wesley Longman.

See especially chapter 1, on the research foundations of content-based instruction, and chapter 32, "The Role of Content in Task-Based EAP Instruction."

Contributor

Sharon Seymour (sharon126@aol.com) received her BA in history and English from Bucknell University and her MA in TESL from San Francisco State University, in the United States. She has been with the ESL department at City College of San Francisco since 1974 and has been chair of the department since 1997.

13 Moving Into the Unknown: When Leaving a Secure Position Sustains Your Professionalism

Susan Conrad

Narrative

Applause broke out around me. I tried to look appreciative rather than embarrassed. It was the final staff meeting of the year in the English department at Iowa State University, and the chair had just announced the promotion decisions for the year. I had been promoted and tenured, and my colleagues were pleased. Then, less than 5 minutes later, there was an awkward pause. Now I did look embarrassed. The chair of the department had just announced who had resigned from Iowa State, and I was on that list, too.

This scenario is not what most people envision in an academic career: Get tenured at a well-respected university with a strong TESL program and immediately leave for a new position, leaving tenure behind. The traditional expectation is that if we are lucky enough to have a position with tenure, we have employment for life, security, and some acknowledgment of our accomplishments by our colleagues and institution. In fact, I was pleased by the decision at Iowa State; however, I was not excited and invigorated about my profession when I thought of being tenured and promoted. I was excited and invigorated at the thought of leaving Iowa State and moving to a less well-known program at Portland State University.

Description

Many TESOL professionals are forced to move to a new job when a short-term position ends or for a variety of other reasons. Although such forced moves may stimulate professional growth, this article addresses a different situation: a voluntary move when you have a good, secure position but want to find one that suits you even more.

Voluntary moves can take place in many contexts. You might make a drastic change in positions within the same institution. For example, I once moved from teaching ESL in an intensive English program to being an administrator in a study abroad program, acquiring new colleagues, a new supervisor, new students, and new job duties. You might move to a new location but continue in a similar type of job, as I did when I moved from teaching English in Korea to teaching ESL in Washington State. You might leave a job to go back to school and obtain training for a new type of position, such as when I left an ESL position for a PhD program. Or, as in my most recent move, you might leave a tenured university position for a new position across the country.

Each of my moves has involved many nerve-racking moments, occasionally making me ask myself, "Why did I ever leave? It would have been so much easier to have stayed!" In many ways it is easier not to move, but looking back over almost 20 years in the TESOL profession, I see that each move has been crucial for keeping me fresh professionally.

Leaving a known, secure position and moving to a new job encourages professional development in numerous ways. Below are five major changes that I have appreciated in all my moves. I illustrate them with examples from my transition from Iowa State to Portland State.

1. new expectations. In a new position, you may be asked to develop skills you did not need in your previous position or play a role you never imagined for yourself. For example, in the

English department at Iowa State, obtaining grants was not considered a priority. At Portland State, in the Department of Applied Linguistics, all of us are expected to pursue grant opportunities. With this expectation, I conceive of my work in new ways—synthesizing what had been separate research areas into a larger cohesive project, developing more opportunities for student researchers, and creating more of a research community.

2. teaching and course development. Different types of students, different courses to teach, maybe even different lengths for terms force you to try new things rather than relying on the known. To take just one example, terms are shorter at Portland State than at Iowa State. This difference has meant that I must reassess the importance of materials and redesign syllabuses even for courses I have previously taught. Shorter terms also mean being able to offer more courses, so I have developed some new, more specialized courses in my primary areas of interest.

3. new perspectives. After a length of time in the same position in the same place, just as with the culture we grow up in, you sometimes forget that there are entirely different ways of doing things. Moving to a new position can be like moving to a new culture. You get new perspectives on problem solving. For example, at Portland State we have begun experimenting with new ways of meeting the diverse research needs of students, offering a sequence of required and elective modules rather than a single research design course.

4. quality of life. Happiness with what you do outside of work can have a large impact on how happy you are professionally. One of the reasons I left Iowa State was because the location did not allow me to pursue my favorite leisure activities. As I moved, I felt rather shallow admitting that mountains and the ocean were important in my decision, but I was right to consider them. Although I have no additional leisure time in Portland, I am more refreshed by my environment because I can more easily do the things I enjoy and, as a consequence, I am happier spending time at work.

5. salary and other benefits. TESOL professionals do not often talk about salaries, and, surely, no one has gone into TESOL to become rich. Furthermore, salaries and benefits can be hard to compare in different locations because cost of living varies greatly. Nevertheless, having my contributions acknowledged with a good pay raise or some other benefit boosts my professional self-esteem. Besides a higher salary, benefits can include a decreased teaching load, support for summer research, a graduate assistant, new computer equipment, or other means of facilitating your work.

Steps

Voluntarily moving from a secure position is different from looking for a position when you do not have one. When you are looking for a first position after finishing a degree, for example, the steps seem relatively clear: You check job listings, send application materials, have interviews, consider your choices, and decide. When you already have a secure position, you may decide not to move at all. You have more to lose, so the process becomes more complex.

The process of looking for a better position as an established professional is more circular. It may take a few years to find a better position. Meanwhile, you may come to assess your current position differently, your personal circumstances may change, or you may decide that your priorities have shifted. The following steps are not a fixed sequence but a list of considerations that I have found important in assessing and reassessing my situation throughout the decision-making process.

1. Know how good you have it and what you are willing to give up. No position is perfect, and you need to know what will make moving worth it. For example, I was willing to move to a university with a less well-established research profile and a lesser known TESOL faculty in order to live in the western United States. On the other hand, I was not willing to give up time to do my research or to move to a place that did not have active, energetic colleagues.

2. Be sure that moving is what you need. Moving changes your circumstances. It may change the specific problems you face, but it does not change you or the fact that there will be problems to face. If a particular problem, such as an argument with a colleague, makes you think you want to move, consider whether you could better spend your time and energy working out your differences with the colleague.

3. Do not worry about what other people think should make you happy. Everyone has different criteria for a fulfilling position. For example, many people were shocked that I would even consider moving from Iowa State to Portland State, a university many people had never even heard of. It was, in fact, a difficult decision because I was treated well and had excellent colleagues and students at Iowa State. However, when I honestly considered my priorities for a long-term position, there were too many disadvantages to staying at Iowa State.

4. Use the usual job-search sources and more. The major sources of job ads, such as the *Chronicle of Higher Education*, the Modern Language Association Job List, and TESOL (see the Resources section), can be useful for finding positions at any level in and outside the United States. However, personal contacts in the field are also important. When programs have an opening for an established professional rather than a recent graduate, they may encourage specific individuals to apply, so it helps to be known in your area of expertise. In addition, get to know other programs and find out which ones are expecting to hire in the near future even if they are not yet advertising.

5. Investigate positions that sound intriguing even if the program is not well known. A program that is unfamiliar may turn out to be a wonderful match for you, or it may be developing in a new, exciting way. I almost decided not to investigate Portland State because I had never heard about its TESOL program. As I investigated, I became increasingly impressed. Researching a place, applying, and interviewing are time consuming, but they are the only means of getting to know a place well enough to make a decision about moving to it.

6. Stay committed to the job search and your current position. Because you may decide to stay in your current job, stay engaged in it while you explore other opportunities. I personally found this to be one of the most challenging aspects of the moving process. It led to the embarrassing situation of being promoted and tenured the same year that I resigned. I had also applied for a sabbatical at Iowa State that year. At times I found it difficult to stay focused because I was considering several possibilities for the next year. However, had the Portland State position not come through, I would have been happy that I had made plans at Iowa State.

7. Take the plunge. You will probably never know with absolute certainty that a new position will be better; you will ultimately just have to decide. You can visit a place, talk to as many people as possible, and gather as much information as you can, but you cannot know exactly what living and working in a new place will be like, especially because relationships with colleagues and roles within a program develop over time. This point was driven home for me when a student at Iowa State stopped by my office after hearing that I would be leaving. She was understanding but said, rather wistfully, "Well, you're well loved here." I realized that she had hit on my biggest fear in moving: What if I was not well loved in my new position? What if I did not love it? None of my information gathering and list making, prodigious as it was, could answer those basic questions.

Conclusion

Moving into the unknown is always somewhat frightening. Moving to a new place is a huge disruption to a career. Moving means learning a whole new system. The first time I wanted to copy an article in the Portland State library, it took me 30 minutes of preliminary work involving maps, change machines, library staff, and copy cards. When you move, even simple tasks become complex, and complex tasks, such as getting new computer equipment set up, can take weeks. When you already have a secure position, moving to a new one is a time-consuming, anxiety-producing process. If you just need a change of pace, take a vacation instead.

On the other hand, staying in a position simply because it is known and secure is not worthwhile if that means resigning yourself to having a job you do not find fulfilling or living in a place that you dislike. When you make a good move, the tiring, anxious times are far outweighed by feelings of invigoration and exhilaration.

Resources

Chronicle of Higher Education. http://www.chronicle.com
> Many institutions of higher education, mostly in the United States, advertise positions in the *Chronicle.* You can browse the listings on the Web site or get a subscription.

JobFinder. http://tesol.jobcontrolcenter.com
> TESOL's JobFinder service helps job seekers find ESL/EFL teaching positions and teacher education faculty positions within and outside of the United States. On the Web site you can view job listings and subscribe to TESOL's *Placement E-Bulletin* of employment opportunities.

Modern Language Association. (n.d.). *MLA job information list.* Retrieved February 10, 2003, from http://www.mla.org /main_jil.htm
> The MLA job list covers mostly U.S. university positions, including English, foreign language, and linguistics. The list comes out four times a year, with the October listing being the largest.

Contributor

Susan Conrad (conrads@pdx.edu) is an associate professor in the Department of Applied Linguistics, at Portland State University, in the United States. Her various moves during her TESOL career have taken her to Africa, Korea, and around the United States, and have included teaching in high school, community college, intensive English programs, a study abroad program, and universities.

14 A Fulbright Adventure: Just Do It!

Gayle Nelson

Narrative

It was twilight. A fine dust was settling on the cars and falling lightly on our heads. The world was silent, the silence of a first snow or an early morning mist. We walked slowly and in wonder. Finally, I said, "It's ash from Popocatepetl [an active volcano nearby]." My 15-year-old son nodded. We walked on, at peace, without saying a word until we reached our *casita* (small house).

Moments like these are rare between mothers and 15-year-old sons (at least in my experience in the United States). But in Mexico, where I spent a year as a Fulbright scholar, my son and I experienced many such moments. You may be wondering what the relationship is between a memorable evening with a son and professional development. In Mexico, my personal and professional lives were inextricably related, and that year continues to affect who I am and what I do—professionally.

Description

When I was hired for a tenure-track position at Georgia State University (GSU), I was enthusiastic, energized, and ready to work. Six years later, when I was promoted and tenured, I was pleased that my hard work and late nights had been rewarded, but I was also exhausted. This feeling is not uncommon, and some academics take sabbaticals, change jobs, or move into administration to overcome it. I, however, needed to get back to what first drew me to ESL as a profession; I needed to go abroad.

Before I started working at GSU, I had lived abroad for 10 years, first as a teenager in high school and later as an adult teaching English. While teaching EFL in the 1980s, my *self* multiplied. I became a historian, an archeologist, an anthropologist, a political scientist, a sociologist, an adventurer, a tour guide, and a reader of literature in translation—in addition to being a teacher. These activities contributed to my professional as well as my personal development. As I was learning the history, politics, literature, and culture of where I was living, I was also learning about the students I was teaching. This focus on students and their cultures influenced my selection of a doctoral program.

When I returned to the United States, I chose intercultural communication for my doctoral work. The issue of cultural factors related to the learning and teaching of English has been my main academic interest and has informed my research and teaching at GSU. However, after 6 years, I needed to go abroad to rediscover my multifaceted self and to return to my professional roots. Numerous programs exist for academics who want to live abroad for a short time and then return (or not) to their home institution. The program I chose, the Fulbright, is one of the better known.

Here is a partial list of what I gained during my Fulbright year.

- I learned a new system. Living in a different country and working in a different university and department means learning a new cultural system. For example, my host institution, La Universidad de las Americas (UDLA), in Puebla, Mexico, closed for lunch between 2 and 4 p.m., students were graded with numbers from 1–10, and female graduate students and female professors often kissed on the cheeks in greeting. At times, the learning was frustrating because the social rules are different and assumed, but if one plays the role of anthropologist and observes and asks, the system becomes comprehensible. International students in the United States go through this process, and EFL instructors who go abroad go through a similar process. It is important for me as a teacher educator to experience this adjustment regularly so I can educate teachers and understand students better.

- I gained new colleagues. I was unprepared for the close relationships I developed with colleagues at the UDLA. They helped me adjust not only to the university and the program, but to Mexico as well. New professional and research collaborations grew, and members of the department and I copresented workshops on Mexican culture for visiting U.S. students, presented papers at MEXTESOL conferences, and conducted research together. Cross-cultural research is difficult without being in the culture one is studying and having researchers from both cultures. Such cross-cultural collaborations would not have happened in Mexico if not for the social bonds created during the year.

- I lived a balanced life. When we arrived in August, I started work, but my son, Jon, had 3 weeks before he started school. I selfishly admit that I was pleased that he had time for me. We did not have a car and became adept at taking buses and taxis to wherever we were going, which was often to the movies. Once Jon made friends, however, he spent less time with me, but we still traveled on weekends, went out to eat, and just talked to each other. We had time to walk silently at twilight and notice the ash falling from the sky.

- I learned from my son. He attended a bilingual Mexican school in Puebla, where he was the only U.S. student. He went to Mexico to play soccer and ended up also learning Spanish, making long-lasting friends, and immersing himself in Mexico. One night I complained that Jorge, another teacher's friend, had promised again and again to fix my computer but never did. Jon looked at me and said, "Mom, he was just being polite." I thought, "I'm the one with a PhD in intercultural communication, and he's teaching me about cultural differences." He continued to be my tutor and social informant throughout our stay.

- I returned renewed. When I returned to GSU in the fall, I taught a graduate course in intercultural communication and received my highest student evaluations ever. I had recently experienced cultural adjustment and could talk authentically about it, and I was experiencing the difficulties of reentry. I also had fresh ideas for research, wrote a grant with a former Mexican graduate student, and have since published the results (Nelson, Lutenbacher, & Lopéz, 2001).

- I maintained contacts. The next summer I taught again at the UDLA, and my son went along to visit friends. The following December, three of his friends spent a month with us in Atlanta. Last summer, my son went to St. Paul, Minnesota, to visit two of these friends, who were studying in an intensive English program. I continue to advise MA theses, attend the oral defenses, and present papers at MEXTESOL conventions.

Steps

The decision to leave Atlanta for a full academic year was not an easy one. My husband could not take a leave from his position. Our son had lived with us as a young child in Egypt for 4 years, and we had hoped to live abroad again before he left home for college, but we were concerned about uprooting a teenager from his school and friends.

We had a good year, but expectations differ from person to person. The following points may help you prepare for your Fulbright year.

1. Know yourself. How well do you deal with the unknown? How comfortable are you with ambiguity? Does it bother you if the mail does not always arrive or if things do not get done as quickly as you would like? How well do you adjust to different value and belief systems? Does it bother you to be alone? Does it bother you to be surrounded by others? I found that at first I

enjoyed having time to myself to explore and read, but soon I became lonely and missed my husband. One of the reasons we chose Mexico as my Fulbright destination was so he could visit often.

2. Know your family. Many families have taken children abroad and have had miserable years. Taking a 15-year-old to a new country where he would need to speak Spanish was a risk, especially since he had had only 1 year of high school Spanish. I also knew that he really wanted to go (an extremely important factor) and that he was a gregarious young man who would learn a foreign language not in a classroom but from interacting with others (if he were to learn one at all). My husband wanted us to go because he knew I needed to and because he wanted our son to go. He is also more self-sufficient than most people I know, but we all were lonely at times. We had large phone bills and were grateful for the Internet.

3. Get the Fulbright application well in advance. The process of applying takes time. As soon as the materials were available, we looked at the Fulbright opportunities for TESOL, narrowed our choices, and talked as a family about the various possibilities. By the time I submitted my application, I had visited the university and received a letter of invitation from the chair of the department, which I submitted with the application to the Fulbright Program.

4. Check out the location. A friend at the UDLA arranged for me to visit the department and present a paper. In this way I met the other faculty members; saw the campus, the type of housing we would be living in, and the many soccer games on campus; talked to parents about secondary schools, visited the schools, and picked up applications. I might have been less cautious had I been going by myself to a new setting, but I wanted to be as sure as possible that Jon would be safe, comfortable, and, I hoped, happy. If you do not have a contact, work the network; find and talk to someone who has been there recently.

5. Make arrangements with your home institution. Soon after you become interested in applying for a Fulbright, talk to your

department chair and dean about financial and insurance matters as well as options for finding a temporary replacement for your position.

6. Find out what you need to bring. This step may seem obvious, but one U.S. visiting scholar brought clothes for warm weather to Puebla, which is more than 7,000 feet above sea level and is cool in the evenings during the summer and cold in the winter. Also find out what you will be teaching so you can bring appropriate books and other materials with you.

7. Make reservations and go. In mid-August, Jon and I flew to Mexico City, then took a bus to Puebla and two taxis (to carry our footlockers) to the campus in the small town of Cholula. By the time we reached the university and found the department, I had started to cry, wondering what on earth we were doing. The department chair suggested I call my husband (and I did) and then took us, and our luggage, to our *casita*. After we brought the footlockers and suitcases into the house, we realized we were hungry. We found a small restaurant, ordered pizza, and watched an episode of the popular U.S. series, *The Simpsons*, on TV in Spanish, eating without talking. By the time we walked back to the university, it had started to rain, and at the gate we could not remember which way to go. Jon suggested one way and I the other. We went my way and walked almost 2 miles before finding our house; if we had gone Jon's way, we would have walked only two blocks. I learned that night to trust my son.

Conclusion

This chapter began with a mother and son walking silently as volcanic ash lightly covered them. It ended with an unpleasant walk in the rain, mother and son full of anxiety that neither expressed. In chronological time, the order was reversed. We were anxious in the beginning. I had no idea what the year would bring. I did not know that Jon's Spanish would surpass mine within 5 months; that he would return to the UDLA 2 years later and take content courses at the university in Spanish; or that he would decide to major in international relations in college. I did not know that I would find my multiple selves again; that I would make friends that I cherish; or that I would return to GSU renewed and pleased to be back. I did not know that my son and I would develop a relationship that would enable us to walk in silence and be at peace with each other. My Fulbright experience did not end after 1 year. It continues still.

Resources

Nelson, G., Lutenbacher, C., & Lopéz, M. (2001). A cross-cultural study of education in Mexico and the United States: Focus on the role of the teacher. *Journal of Multilingual and Multicultural Matters, 22,* 463–474.

U.S. Department of State, Bureau of Educational and Cultural Affairs. (n.d.). *The Fulbright program.* Retrieved February 10, 2003, from http://exchanges.state.gov/education/fulbright

This site includes information about various Fulbright programs and the application procedures.

Contributor

Gayle Nelson (gaylenelson@gsu.edu), professor and department chair, teaches master's and doctoral students in the Department of Applied Linguistics and ESL at Georgia State University, in the United States. Her primary areas of interest are the multiple roles of culture in language teaching and learning, cultural considerations in the teaching of L2 writing, and academic writing. She has lived or taught in Turkey, Uganda, Kuwait, Egypt, and Mexico.

15 Starting a TESOL Caucus for Nonnative Speakers of English: The Politics of Professional Development

George Braine

Narrative

Growing up in Ceylon (now Sri Lanka) in the 1950s and 1960s, I read widely in English, including local newspapers and magazines published in the United States, such as *Reader's Digest* and *Time*, as well as those distributed for free by the United States Information Agency. Although the U.S. magazines were glossy and attractively designed, with colorful illustrations and eye-catching advertisements, the articles in the local newspapers were as well written as any in the U.S. magazines.

In the secondary school I attended, I was taught English by local as well as expatriate British teachers. The local teachers were impeccable speakers of English, whose love of the language shone through in their enthusiasm for teaching it. Other than skin color and accent, I could not discern a difference between the teachers who were nonnative speakers of English and those who were native speakers. This pattern was repeated at the teachers college I attended later. In fact, all the local lecturers there had more teaching experience and some, with graduate degrees from prestigious British and U.S. universities, were more qualified than the single expatriate lecturer.

However, in the Middle East, where I taught in the early 1980s, I first became aware of the low status of nonnative-English-speaking (NNS) teachers because teachers from Britain, some with a mere 3- or 6-month teaching certificate, were paid higher salaries and enjoyed better perks than well-qualified teachers from the Indian subcontinent. But the native-nonnative distinction hit me with full force only when I arrived in the United States and began graduate school in 1984. With more than a decade of experience as an English teacher under my belt, I applied for a tutor position at the university's language center and was turned down almost instantly. Instead, native-English-speaking (NS) classmates who had no teaching experience were hired. I shelved books in the library for minimum wage while my classmates tutored at the language center.

Description

The professional development of many in our field depends to a great extent on their access to education and work. Becoming politically active concerning more equal access, or for any cause, can improve our profession and stimulate our own professional development as we network, publish, present, organize, and foster change. I survived graduate school and managed to overcome the open prejudice that existed in the 1980s against the hiring of nonnative speakers as English teachers, but I continued to be bothered by the fact that most issues of concern to nonnative speakers in TESOL continued to be overlooked.

To bring more visibility to these issues, I organized a colloquium, titled *In Their Own Voices: Nonnative Speaker Professionals in TESOL*, at the 1996 TESOL convention, held in Chicago. The highly charged, mainly personal narratives of the speakers (including Ulla Connor, Suresh Canagarajah, and Kamal Sridhar) generated much interest and enthusiasm among nonnative speakers in the audience. Some attendees claimed that they finally had a voice within TESOL. The colloquium has been widely influential, spawning other colloquia at subsequent TESOL conventions and inspiring an anthology, *Non-Native Educators in English Language Teaching* (Braine, 1999). The idea for a TESOL caucus for nonnative speakers was first proposed at the colloquium.

The proposed caucus received an unexpected boost when Alexander Jenin (1998), a nonnative speaker of English, wrote an article for *TESOL Matters* detailing the prejudices he faced in finding employment as an English teacher. I was invited to write a companion piece to his article. My article (Braine, 1998), on invisible barriers in English language teaching, was published under the big, bold headline "Nonnative Speakers and ELT." In the article, I pointed out that qualifications, ability, and experience were of little help to many NNS teachers in the job market, where the invisible rule appeared to be *No NNS teachers need apply*. Despite the TESOL organization's explicit opposition to hiring practices that discriminate against NNS teachers, most English language teaching administrators (with some notable exceptions) did not hire NNS teachers. I described two excuses trotted out for not hiring these individuals:

1. ESL students prefer being taught by NS teachers.

2. Recruiting foreigners involves a complex legal process.

I also wrote, however, that the main reason, though never explicitly stated, was the increasing presence of NNS professionals in Western academia as teachers, researchers, and scholars in almost every discipline, including English language teaching. Although this change is only to be expected—there are at least four NNS ESOL professionals to every NS one—there was resentment among NNS candidates, who were competing for scarce jobs. I argued that this resentment was especially ironic in the field of English language teaching, considering the profession's strident championing of multiculturalism, diversity, and other sociopolitical causes, often on behalf of ESL students and immigrants. Although ESL students are praised and admired for the multiculturalism and diversity they bring to language classes, NNS teachers, who can also contribute their rich multicultural, multilingual experiences, are often barred from the same classes.

I pointed out another irony. When NNS teachers return to their countries after qualifying in the West, they cannot always find work. Some language program administrators, notably in Japan, Korea, and Hong Kong, prefer to hire unqualified NS teachers instead of qualified locals. I stated that Jenin and others like him were in the bewildering and frustrating position of being denied what they have been trained to do. I advised NNS readers that they would have to accept the fact that the playing field would not be level for them and struggle twice as hard to achieve what often comes as a birthright to their NS counterparts: recognition of their teaching ability and respect for their scholarship. I reminded them that, often, teaching ability alone would not be enough for obtaining employment or for career advancement. They had to grow as professionals, taking active roles and assuming leadership in teacher organizations, initiating research, sharing their ideas through publications, and learning to network with NNS colleagues. They would meet courageous administrators who would see beyond their accents and pronunciation, mentors who would promote their careers, and colleagues who would support their research and publication efforts.

The article evoked immediate, mostly positive reactions from NS as well as NNS teachers from around the world. Once again, some teachers told me that what they had known all along (i.e., about the prejudices they faced in the job market and at work) had finally been stated openly.

In spite of the high level of attention and broad support from teachers, efforts to establish a TESOL caucus for NNS teachers did not proceed smoothly. We only needed the signatures of 200 TESOL members to petition the organization for a provisional caucus. We prepared signature forms and collected signatures at the 1997 TESOL convention, in Orlando, Florida. We also mailed forms to supporters in and outside the United States, asking them to obtain signatures from their colleagues. Jun Liu of the University of Arizona and Lía Kamhi-Stein of California State University, Los Angeles, were at the forefront of signature collection, working tirelessly to publicize our cause and gather signatures. At the 1997 TESOL convention, I clearly remember Liu soliciting attendees in the hallways and at various presentations.

Although we collected the required number of signatures, we soon discovered that many people who had signed our petition were not members of TESOL and that their support would not be useful to the establishment of our caucus. We therefore had to redouble our efforts. Finally, in 1998, we established the caucus under my leadership. The caucus met formally for the first time at the 1999 TESOL convention, in New York City, which coincided with the launch of my book, *Non-Native Educators in English Language Teaching* (Braine, 1999). The overall aim of the caucus is to strengthen effective teaching and learning of English around the world while respecting individuals' language rights. Specifically, the major goals are to

- create a nondiscriminatory professional environment for all TESOL members, regardless of native language and place of birth
- encourage formal and informal gatherings of nonnative speakers at TESOL and affiliate conferences
- encourage research and publications on the role of NNS teachers in ESL and EFL contexts
- promote the role of NNS members in TESOL and affiliate leadership positions

Steps

I offer the following advice to TESOL professionals as they explore ways of sustaining and energizing their careers and of seeking to improve the world.

1. Communicate your concerns to other professionals. Find out how widespread the problems may be. Study the situation, the causes, and possible solutions.

2. Use your organizations to communicate more broadly. Organize presentations, colloquia, and special-topic issues of journals; submit a TESOL resolution; and use other communication mechanisms (e.g., Web sites, electronic discussion lists, e-mail) offered by the profession. You never know what activity might motivate others to become involved, so try many. For example, when I organized the TESOL colloquium back in 1996, I had no plans to start a caucus for nonnative speakers. The movement to start a caucus came from others, and it soon acquired a life of its own.

3. Learn to recognize a good idea. When the caucus was proposed, the question was asked, "How could a TESOL caucus help the cause of NNS teachers?" I realized that the cause could be better

served within the TESOL organization and recognized that the proposal was a sound idea that needed to be pursued and promoted.

4. Do not underestimate the power of a good idea. Despite the obstacles described above, the caucus became a reality within 2 years of the 1996 colloquium. The idea fired the imaginations of a number of enthusiastic and talented TESOL members, and there was no stopping it.

5. Learn to identify reliable supporters early. When campaigning for a cause, the successful outcome depends not only on the legitimacy and popularity of the cause, but also on the active and committed support of others. I was able to recognize a few such supporters early, and we worked as a team to promote the caucus.

6. Learn to accept disappointment. Just as some enthusiasts will support and promote your ideas throughout a campaign, others will drift away for various reasons. This wavering support might lead you to doubt the worthiness of your cause, but learning to accept the fact that you cannot convince everyone all the time will help you sustain your own enthusiasm.

7. Network. Even though you may have support for a cause at the grassroots level, it is difficult to succeed without the support of those in leadership positions. Networking is therefore essential to the success of any campaign.

8. Publicize and organize. To reach our goal of establishing a TESOL caucus, we quickly established a caucus Web site (managed by Aya Matsuda, at the University of New Hampshire) and posted a bibliography of publications relating to NNS issues. So far, the caucus has published eight newsletters. We also encouraged members to write for TESOL serial publications (e.g., *TESOL Matters*, *TESOL Quarterly*, and *TESOL Journal*) to spotlight NNS issues. We put forward proposals for presentations, colloquia, and workshops at TESOL conventions and succeeded in getting many of the proposals accepted. We also initiated a program for aspiring leaders of the caucus so that, over a 3-year period, they would

begin as the newsletter editor, then become incoming chair, then assume the role of the caucus chair.

Conclusion

To a large extent, we have achieved our goals. As I write this chapter, I have in hand Vol. 4, No. 1 of the 12-page caucus newsletter, edited by chair-elect Paul Matsuda of the University of New Hampshire, which includes a section on "Caucus Events at the Upcoming TESOL 2002." Thirteen events are listed, ranging from individual presentations to colloquia and workshops. The topics also range widely, from the preparation of NNS teachers in and outside the United States to publishing strategies. The presenters are from a variety of countries, including Taiwan, Kazakhstan, Lithuania, Hong Kong, Singapore, the United Arab Emirates, and, of course, the United States.

When I decided to leave the United States in 1995 and build a career in Hong Kong, I realized that it would not be easy to inhabit both worlds. Hong Kong has a vibrant English language teaching community that has little to do with the TESOL organization in the United States because Hong Kong's close ties to Britain pervade many areas, including English language teaching. Nonetheless, my ties to the United States were too strong to relinquish, and I continue to attend TESOL conventions, organize colloquia, and write for U.S. publications. In the early years, the caucus helped and inspired me to sustain my ties to the United States, ties that have strengthened over the years. My reward has been to see what began as a colloquium in 1996 grow rapidly into a dynamic force within TESOL.

Resources

Braine, G. (1998, February/March). NSS [sic] and invisible barriers in ELT. *TESOL Matters, 8*(1), 14.

Braine, G. (1999). *Non-native educators in English language teaching.* Mahwah, NJ: Erlbaum.

Jenin, A. (1998, February/March). I wish a [sic] had heard a different story. *TESOL Matters, 8*(1), 14.

TESOL. (n.d.). *Non-Native English Speakers in TESOL caucus.* Retrieved February 12, 2003, from http://www.unh.edu/nnest/

The official home page of the Nonnative English Speakers in TESOL caucus includes a link (by clicking on "History") to the *TESOL Matters* article "NSS and Invisible Barriers in ELT" (Braine, 1998).

Contributor

George Braine (georgebraine@cuhk.edu.hk), who is Sri Lankan, is an associate professor of English at the Chinese University of Hong Kong. He is editor of *Teaching English to the World*, published by TESOL.

Users' Guide to Strands in the Professional Development in Language Education Series

Chapters are categorized by their main strands only.

Administration and Organization

Collaborative Development for Teachers, Students, and Cultures

Volume 1

Volume 2

Volume 3

Computer Technology and Networking

Observation of and Reflection in Teaching and Research

On the Move

Publishing

Volume 2

12 Creating Publishing Communities (Tim Murphey, Mark Connolly, Eton Churchill, John McLaughlin, Susan L. Schwartz, and Jarek Krajka; creating and editing accessible publications for teacher and researcher development)

Volume 3

5 Writing for Grant Dollar$ (Jane E. Averill)
6 The Roller Coaster Ride of Editing a Book (John M. Murphy)
7 Small Corrections: Becoming a Textbook Writer (Linda Grant)

Research and Presenting

Volume 1

3 In the Limelight: Presenting to Your Peers (Maureen Snow Andrade)

Volume 2

1 Long-Distance Collaboration: Rescuing Each Other From the Desert Island (Angela Beck and Joy Janzen)
4 Fostering Graduate School Teacher Development Through Peer Interviewing (Greta Gorsuch and David Beglar)
5 Pulp Fiction? The Research Journal and Professional Development (Simon Borg)

Volume 3

2 Becoming "Scholar of the College" (Andrew D. Cohen)
12 Sabbatical Projects Can Make a Difference: A Tale of Curriculum Revision (Sharon Seymour)

Teacher Education

Volume 2

10 Thais That Bind: Becoming a Teacher Educator Through International Volunteering (Susan Carbery and Robert Croker)
11 Starting a Local Teacher Study Group (Kazuyoshi Sato)

Volume 3

Volunteerism, Advocacy, and Politics _____

Volume 1

Volume 2

Volume 3

Also Available From TESOL

Academic Writing Programs
Ilona Leki, Editor

Action Research
Julian Edge, Editor

Bilingual Education
Donna Christian and Fred Genesee, Editors

Community Partnerships
Elsa Auerbach, Editor

Content-Based Instruction in Higher Education Settings
JoAnn Crandall and Dorit Kaufman, Editors

Distance-Learning Programs
Lynn E. Henrichsen, Editor

Grammar Teaching in Teacher Education
Dilin Liu and Peter Master, Editors

*Implementing the ESL Standards for Pre-K–12 Students
Through Teacher Education*
Marguerite Ann Snow, Editor

*Integrating the ESL Standards Into Classroom Practice:
Grades Pre-K–2*
Betty Ansin Smallwood, Editor

*Integrating the ESL Standards Into Classroom Practice:
Grades 3–5*
Katharine Davies Samway, Editor

*Integrating the ESL Standards Into Classroom Practice:
Grades 6–8*
Suzanne Irujo, Editor

Integrating the ESL Standards Into Classroom Practice:
Grades 9–12
Barbara Agor, Editor

Intensive English Programs in Postsecondary Settings
Nicholas Dimmitt and Maria Dantas-Whitney, Editors

Interaction and Language Learning
Jill Burton and Charles Clennell, Editors

Internet for English Teaching
Mark Warschauer, Heidi Shetzer, and Christine Meloni

Journal Writing
Jill Burton and Michael Carroll, Editors

Mainstreaming
Effie Papatzikou Cochran

PACE Yourself: A Handbook for ESL Tutors
Teresa S. Dalle and Laurel J. Young

Teacher Education
Karen E. Johnson, Editor

Technology-Enhanced Learning Environments
Elizabeth Hanson-Smith, Editor

For more information, contact
Teachers of English to Speakers of Other Languages, Inc.
700 South Washington Street, Suite 200
Alexandria, Virginia 22314 USA
Tel 703-836-0774 • Fax 703-836-6447 • publications@tesol.org
• http://www.tesol.org/